# CUCINA DELL'EMILIA-ROMAGNA

# CUCINA DELL'EMILIA-ROMAGNA

RECIPES FROM THE GASTRONOMIC HEARTLAND OF ITALY AND ITS CAPITAL BOLOGNA

Ursula Ferrigno

photography by RITA PLATTS

RYLAND PETERS & SMALL

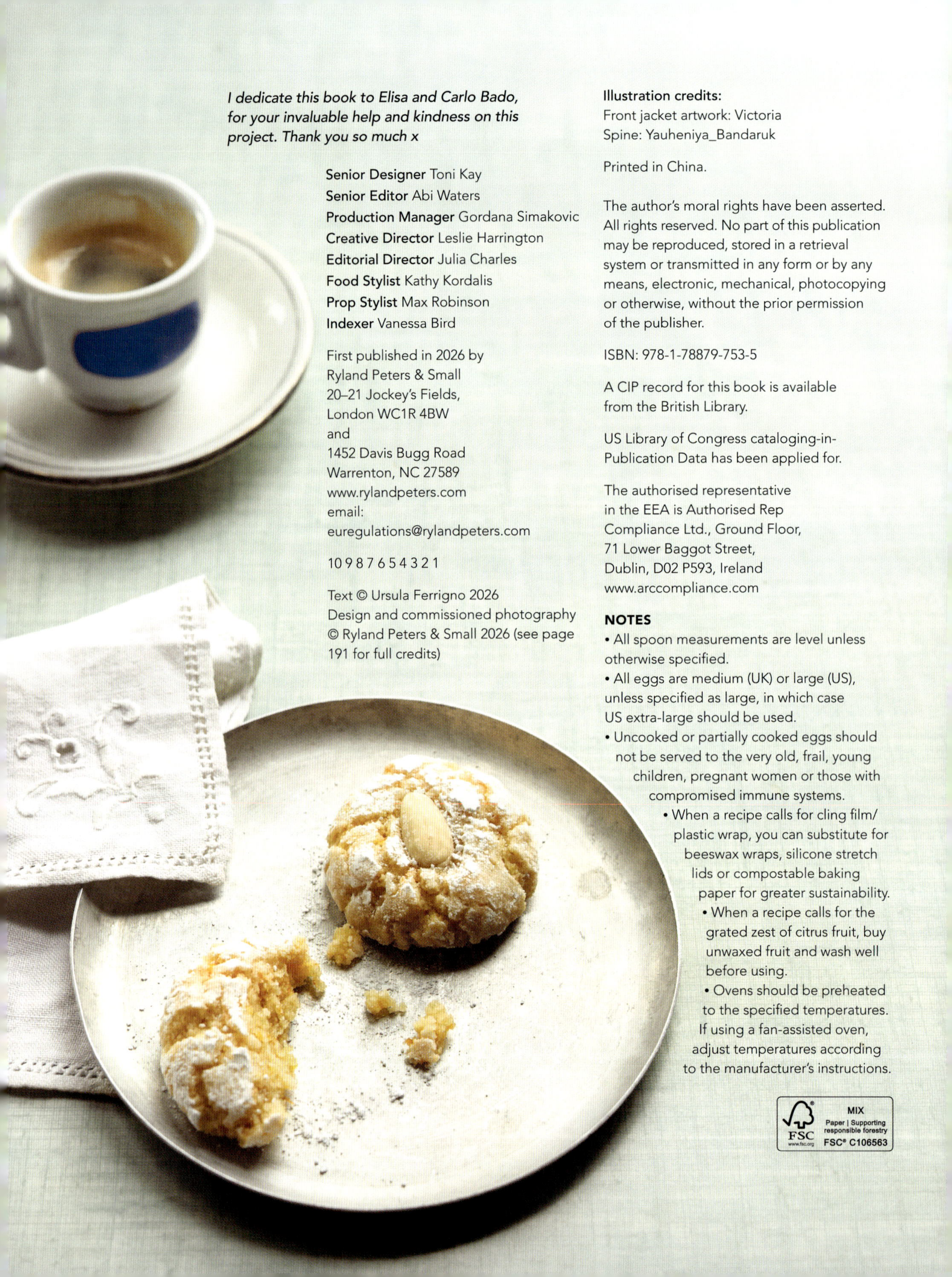

*I dedicate this book to Elisa and Carlo Bado, for your invaluable help and kindness on this project. Thank you so much x*

**Senior Designer** Toni Kay
**Senior Editor** Abi Waters
**Production Manager** Gordana Simakovic
**Creative Director** Leslie Harrington
**Editorial Director** Julia Charles
**Food Stylist** Kathy Kordalis
**Prop Stylist** Max Robinson
**Indexer** Vanessa Bird

First published in 2026 by
Ryland Peters & Small
20–21 Jockey's Fields,
London WC1R 4BW
and
1452 Davis Bugg Road
Warrenton, NC 27589
www.rylandpeters.com
email:
euregulations@rylandpeters.com

10 9 8 7 6 5 4 3 2 1



**Illustration credits:**
Front jacket artwork: Victoria
Spine: Yauheniya_Bandaruk

Printed in China.



ISBN: 978-1-78879-753-5

A CIP record for this book is available from the British Library.

US Library of Congress cataloging-in-Publication Data has been applied for.

The authorised representative in the EEA is Authorised Rep Compliance Ltd., Ground Floor, 71 Lower Baggot Street, Dublin, D02 P593, Ireland
www.arccompliance.com

**NOTES**

- All spoon measurements are level unless otherwise specified.
- All eggs are medium (UK) or large (US), unless specified as large, in which case US extra-large should be used.
- Uncooked or partially cooked eggs should not be served to the very old, frail, young children, pregnant women or those with compromised immune systems.
- When a recipe calls for cling film/ plastic wrap, you can substitute for beeswax wraps, silicone stretch lids or compostable baking paper for greater sustainability.
- When a recipe calls for the grated zest of citrus fruit, buy unwaxed fruit and wash well before using.
- Ovens should be preheated to the specified temperatures. If using a fan-assisted oven, adjust temperatures according to the manufacturer's instructions.

# CONTENTS

# THE EPICENTRE OF ITALIAN CUISINE

**Emilia-Romagna is one of the wealthiest and most developed regions in Italy. It is a major cultural centre, with many ancient cities, architectural and natural marvels, and numerous UNESCO World Heritage Sites. It is also the prime gastronomic region of Italy as it produces so many world-famous foods, among them Parma ham and Parmigiano Reggiano. Here, people think, talk and fantasize about food more than anywhere else in Italy. From morning to night, they ask each other what they are going to eat that day, precisely how they will prepare it, and what they will serve to accompany it.**

## EMILIA & ROMAGNA

Emilia-Romagna, as it is today, is divided into nine provinces: from the west, Piacenza, Parma, Reggio Emilia, Modena, Bologna, Ferrara, Ravenna, Forlì-Cesena and Rimini. The regional capital is Bologna.

Emilia and Romagna are two distinct areas within the conjoined region of Emilia-Romagna. They both became part of a unified Italy in 1861, but were united administratively in the late 1940s. Emilia lies on the rich and fertile plains of the Po Valley, the Pianura Padana. Romagna has a long Adriatic coastline, the Riviera Romagnola, but much of the land is hilly, rising up to the Apennine mountains.

The people are said to be quite different in character. The Emilians are wealthier and more 'cool' than their neighbours, and their food reflects this. It is subtle, rich and smooth: think of those silky hand-made pastas and cream sauces, that long-braised ragù. The Romagnards, in contrast, are said to be poorer financially, more fiery and outgoing. Their food tends to be less refined, but lighter and cleaner – simply grilled meat and fish, perhaps presented in the famous local piadina bread.

Another difference is that the Romagnards use a lot of olive oil in their cooking – olives are grown in the foothills – while the Emilians tend to use butter (and lard) as their cooking medium. (Indeed, the southern use of olive oil, and the northern of butter, is one of the principal culinary dividing factors in Italy itself.) But another difference is again based on character, and is probably apocryphal! They say that to discover which area you are in, you knock on a door and ask for a drink. If you are in Emilia, you will get a glass of water. If in Romagna, you will be offered wine (a Sangiovese, which is good here).

Where Emilia becomes Romagna, or vice versa, is disputed – the rivers Sillaro and Reno are said to be involved – but the greatest dividing factor in the present-day region is now the SS9 (Strada Statale 9), known familiarly as the Via Emilia. The Romans built this road, which stretched from Rimini in the south-east to Piacenza in the north-west. They built a string of Roman colonies along it, like beads on a necklace, and these 'beads' are known as Bologna, Modena, Reggio Emilia and Parma, each of them still rich in Roman ruins. The road was completed in 187BC, and the *autostrada* of today follows the same route.

Emilia-Romagna is not just famous for its food. Lying along the Via Emilia is 'motor valley', where many luxury car (and tractor) manufacturers are based, among them Ferrari, Lamborghini, Maserati and

*The Piazza Maggiore, with its typical terracotta brick buildings, is the heart of the city of Bologna.*

Ducati. Music and the arts are well represented in the region: Luciano Pavarotti was from Modena, Giuseppe Verdi from Parma; the film directors Federico Fellini from Rimini, and Bernardo Bertolucci from Parma. A food writer much loved in Italy is Pellegrino Artusi: he came from Forlimpopoli, and wrote the first book of cohesive national cuisine in 1891.

**THE BEST IN ITALY**

Even among Italians, who are very loyally regional in their culinary tastes, the food of Emilia-Romagna is considered to be the best in Italy. This is primarily due to simple geography. One of the largest Italian regions, Emilia-Romagna lies between the Adriatic Sea to the east, the River Po to the north and the Apennine mountains to the south. Between the mountains and the Po is what is known as the 'food valley', where a unique microclimate means that an abundance of foods can be produced. These include soft wheat for the famous pasta types of the region; cereals to feed the pigs that produce the countless *salumi* (cold cuts or cured meats) such as Prosciutto di Parma, Mortadella Bologna etc; grape vines, which are used not just in the wines of the area, but in the world-renowned balsamic vinegars of Modena; and cows, which produce the milk for the region's cheeses, particularly Parmigiano Reggiano.

There are 44 individual local food products that have protected status from the EU, more than anywhere else in Italy (or the world). IGP, or 'Protected Geographical Indication', means that the product is linked to a geographical area, but not fully (processing may be elsewhere). DOP, or 'Protected Designation of Origin', ensures that the product has been grown, produced and processed in one area. IGP products in the region include mortadella and piadina, while DOP covers Parmigiano Reggiano, Parma ham and the balsamic vinegars of Modena and Reggio Emilia.

The region has possibly more museums of ingredients than anywhere else in Italy, denoting just how dedicated its inhabitants are to food. Bread is celebrated in Ferrara, piadina in Rimini, olive oil growing in Brisighella, borlenghi, chestnuts and cheese in Zocca, and ice cream in Bologna. Some of the most iconic recipes of the region have actually been registered by the Italian Culinary Academy with the Bologna Chamber of Commerce: most notably the Bolognese ragù, and the filling of tortellini.

Emilia-Romagna's ancient cities are glorious, rich in history and astounding architectural beauty. Ravenna, Parma, Reggio Emilia, Modena and Ferrara have proud food traditions that stretch back through hundreds of years – Parma is actually named the UNESCO Creative City of Gastronomy – but it is Bologna that is closest to my heart. Both the political and gastronomic capital of the region, Bologna has several nicknames: it is called *La Rossa*, the 'red one', because of the colour of its terracotta bricks; it is also known as *La Grassa*, the 'fat one', or indeed the 'rich one', referring both to the culinary richness and the wealth of the city; its designation of *La Dotta*, the 'learned one', refers to it being the home of the oldest university in the western world.

I have explored the basilicas and churches, lingered in the atmospheric Piazza Maggiore, where the Bolognese meet, chat and eat; I have wondered at the glorious foodstuffs on display on the stalls in the cobblestoned Quadrilatero and inside the Mercato di Mezzo; and I have wandered through the city's famous porticoes (although not all of them, they stretch over 60 kilometres!). These porticoes have sheltered people from the sun and rain for hundreds of years, and could be seen as an enduring symbol of the city and its hospitality. Bologna, with its history, beauty, warmth and generosity, encapsulates the essence of Emilia-Romagna, even of Italy herself – *il bel paese*, 'the beautiful country'.

CHAPTER ONE

# APPETIZERS
# Antipasti

*The Castello di Torrechiara nestles among the hills of Parma, an area that is part of Italy's renowned 'food valley' where many world-class ingredients are produced. Located very close to the castle is the town of Langhirano, considered the heart of Prosciutto di Parma production.*

# THE PERFECT START

IN ITALY, ANTIPASTI ARE SERVED as an accompaniment to a pre-lunch or dinner drink, or as the first course of a meal. In general, *antipasti* are small, light and simple dishes that are hugely flavourful, but they must not fill you up too much before the subsequent courses. Experts say that smells of food cooking reach receptors in the nose first and then the brain, which stimulates the production of saliva and gastric juices – this starts the process of digestion before food is even put into the mouth! So the first aromas and flavours of a meal, such as *antipasti*, are vitally important: they should tantalize your taste buds and awaken your appetite.

In Emilia-Romagna, the wonderful pork products and cheeses feature predominantly in antipasti. In restaurants, and at home, a *tagliere misto* (charcuterie plate) might be offered: a platter of sliced local *salumi* (cold cuts or cured meats), such as Prosciutto di Parma, Mortadella Bologna, Coppa Piacentina and Salame di Felino. Prosciutto di Parma or Parma ham probably needs no introduction, so famous has it become throughout the world. It is a raw cured ham, made from the hind legs of the pig; the hams are rubbed daily with salt for a month, then hung in ham 'cathedrals' for at least 12 months, during which the ham loses a considerable proportion of its weight. The pigs are fed on a strict diet of cereal, such as corn and barley, supplemented with whey, a by-product of Parmigiano Reggiano cheese-making, another famous local product (this whey is also made into ricotta cheese). I like to think the pigs might enjoy the occasional acorn or chestnut as well, but I suspect their diets are very strict.

Mortadella Bologna is another *antipasto* platter staple: it is a large sausage made of finely ground pork, which is mixed with cubes of hard pork fat, seasonings and often black peppercorns, coriander seeds or pistachio nuts. The mixture is wrapped in a casing, then cooked. (They say that the sausage used to be made with donkey meat, and indeed a Lazio version is made with horsemeat.) When immigrant Italians introduced mortadella to the United States, the sausage became known as Bologna, which evolved into baloney. Antonio Carluccio's mother used to fry thick slices of mortadella dipped in egg and breadcrumbs, similar to how the British used to cook Spam. Becoming increasingly popular as an *antipasto*, particularly in Bologna, is a mousse, *spuma di mortadella*, made with mortadella, ricotta, Parmigiano Reggiano and cream.

Coppa Piacentina is a cured pork neck salami from Piacenza, the westernmost of the Emilian provinces. The meat is cured for up to six months; it is known for its bright red colour, marbled with fat, and its delicate flavour. Other local *salumi* include Culatello from Zibello, near Modena, Felino from the town and comune with the same name, near Parma, and Salama da Sugo, a very old speciality of Ferrara (often using pig's tongue and liver). Cotechino, a pork sausage found all over Italy, is particularly valued in Emilia-Romagna; cooked and sliced, it can be served as *antipasti*. Salami are also made regionally from boar, deer and horse meat.

On your platter of *tagliere misto*, there might be some cheeses too, such as Parmigiano Reggiano or Grana Padano, Pecorino dell' Appennino Reggiano, Raviggiolo or squacquerone. Parmigiano Reggiano, like Parma ham, needs no introduction, as it has become one of our culinary necessities, loved not just for its flavour, but for its flavour-enhancing properties when grated over pasta or other dishes. You might be lucky enough to find, when in Emilia-Romagna, some *Tosone* cheese: this is a by-product of Parmigiano Reggiano, pieces shaved off when the cheese is being shaped into wheels. At this stage, when the cheese is soft, it is good on an *antipasto* platter. Grana Padano and Pecorino are hard cheeses and, like Parmigiano, are good for grating, while Raviggiolo (sheep's milk) and squacquerone (cow's milk) are soft in texture.

These soft cheeses are ideally accompanied by the breads in the next chapter (see pages 34–65). Try piadine, crescentine or gnocco fritto, the smaller breads most associated with *antipasti*, or any of the more conventional ones, like ciabatta or focaccia. From the mountains, borlenghi, also known as zampanelli, are large thin and crisp pancakes that are served hot, folded, with a typical filling of pesto alla Montanara, also known as cunza or pesto Bolognese, a mixture of lard, garlic, rosemary and grated Parmigiano. (Lard used to be the favoured cooking medium in this porcine region.)

Another *antipasto* popular in Emilia-Romagna is calzagatti, a peasant dish from Modena: a mixture

of beans and polenta is left to set, then fried in small pieces. The name literally means 'cat shoe' – no, I have no idea where that comes from....

Other *antipasti* include vegetables presented in various ways, like on bruschetta, as a tasty salad, or even stuffed in fried sage leaves. You could serve fruit – figs or melon – with some Parma ham. Often whole tarts are made with interesting fillings, which are then cut into smaller pieces or wedges for serving as a starter: I give a typical pastry recipe in this chapter that can be used for both the Courgette Pie (see page 20) and my version of erbazzone. This spinach tart, from Reggio Emilia, consists of pastry layers with a filling of assorted, usually summer greens, pancetta and Parmigiano Reggiano. Pumpkin is another vegetable used in tarts in the region.

Whatever you decide to offer for *antipasti*, please do not forget to add some preserved vegetables to give that essential Italian sweet-and-sour flavour. I have only recently discovered *la giardiniera* (see page 31), from the Parma area, and I have fallen in love. A variety of vegetables are cut into pieces, bottled with a spice mix, then covered with a hot pickling liquid. This relish is the best possible accompaniment to *antipasti* of all sorts. Introduced to Chicago in the late 19th century by Italian immigrants, *la giardiniera* is used on everything: hot dogs, burgers, pizzas, sandwiches and salads.

I had a wonderful *tagliere misto* when in Bologna, at the famous and ancient Tamburini Salsamenteria and La Prosciutteria. Both served a wonderful selection of *salumi* and cheese on wooden boards. And the final *antipasti* accompaniment? A glass of Lambrusco.

# ASSORTED APPETIZERS

## ANTIPASTI ASSORTITI

*This is particularly celebrated in the province of Parma. Meats are always cut fresh and never rolled or folded as that would damage the texture, instead they are delicately and systematically arranged on a plate. If fruit and cheese are accompanying the meats, they are always placed in the centre. See page 14 for more information on putting together a* tagliere misto *(charcuterie plate).*

**1 cantaloupe melon**
**6 fresh figs**
**200 g/7 oz. coppa, thinly sliced**
**200 g/7 oz. salami, thinly sliced**
**200 g/7 oz. pancetta, thinly sliced**
**200 g/7 oz. cotechino, cooked and sliced**
**200 g/7 oz. Prosciutto di Parma, thinly sliced**
**bread, to serve**

**Serves 6–8**

Cut the melon in half, remove the seeds and skin, then cut into thin slices. Arrange the slices next to each other in the centre of a serving platter.

Clean the figs and halve them lengthways. Nestle the figs, flesh side up, among the melon slices.

Arrange the slices of coppa on one section of the platter. Keeping each type of meat separate, do the same with the slices of salami, pancetta, cotechino and Prosciutto di Parma.

Serve with bread, such as Gnocco Fritto (see page 60) or Focaccia con Olive (see page 64).

# FRIED STUFFED SAGE LEAVES

## SALVIA FRITTA

*Another example of simplicity and one of the most requested recipes at my cookery classes. Sage is derived from the Latin* salvus *meaning 'healthy', in reference to its therapeutic properties. It was used by the Egyptians, Romans and Greeks. The latter considered it to be sacred, and offered it to the gods.*

**24 fresh sage leaves**
**12 anchovy fillets in olive oil**
**60 g/½ cup Italian 00 flour**
**90 ml/⅓ cup sparkling water**
**olive oil, for frying**
**lemon wedges, to serve**

**Makes 12**

Place 12 sage leaves face up on a baking sheet. Top each leaf with an anchovy fillet and then cover each anchovy with a similar sized sage leaf facing down. Press the leaves together by placing a second baking sheet on the top and adding weights. Leave to press for about 30 minutes.

While you are waiting, mix the flour and water together using a whisk to make a smooth batter.

When ready to cook, heat the oil in a large frying pan/skillet. Working in small batches, dip the pressed sage leaves into the batter one at a time and carefully lower into the hot oil. Do not overcrowd the pan. Fry the sage leaves until golden on one side, then turn using tongs. Fry on the other side until golden and crispy. Carefully remove from the oil and drain on paper towels. Serve with lemon wedges for squeezing over.

# COURGETTE PIE

## TORTINO DI ZUCCHINE

*Please, for optimum results, always use tender young courgettes/zucchini. This is a wonderful* antipasti *or* contorni *(vegetable side dish).*

**5 young courgettes/ zucchini**
**50 g/3½ tablespoons unsalted butter, softened**
**125 g/scant 1½ cups grated Grana Padano, plus extra for topping**
**2 large/US extra-large free-range eggs**
**1 garlic clove, grated**
**90 g/¾ cup Italian 00 flour**
**handful of fresh flat-leaf parsley, leaves chopped**
**60 g/2 oz. squacquerone (spreadable, soft cow's milk cheese from Romagna)**
**1 tablespoon olive oil**
**salt and freshly ground black pepper**

*32 x 20-cm/13 x 8-inch baking sheet*

**Serves 4–6**

Preheat the oven to 180°C/160°C fan/350°F/ gas 4.

Coarsely grate 4 of the courgettes into a bowl, then thinly slice the remaining courgette and set aside for the topping.

Add the butter, Grana Padano, eggs, garlic, flour, parsley and some salt and pepper to the bowl of grated courgettes and mix well.

Line the baking sheet with parchment paper. Spoon half the grated courgette mixture onto the sheet, then spread it out evenly to the edges. Next, spread the squacquerone in a thin layer over the top. Cover with the remaining grated courgette mixture.

To finish, lay the thin slices of courgette on the surface, drizzle with olive oil and sprinkle over some grated Grana Padano. Bake in the preheated oven for 25 minutes until golden.

Serve cut into squares.

# ROSEMARY & LARDO CRÊPES

## BORLENGHI

*This recipe originates from the coastal town of Cervia in Ravenna. It celebrates the feast day of San Lorenzo. On August 10 each year, local residents immerse themselves in the waters of the Adriatic Sea. The custom dates back to 1927, when an outbreak of malaria occurred in San Lorenzo and the local priest stipulated that the sick should be carried to the beach and immersed in the cold sea water seven times in a single day.*

*I mentioned this recipe to a colleague at Eataly London and she immediately told me how delicious they are. Traditionally made without egg, I tried and failed to get an authentic version of these crêpes working perfectly, so decided to write this recipe with eggs. If you are feeling adventurous, do try the version without eggs (see note below).*

**1 garlic clove**
**1 tablespoon fresh rosemary leaves**
**70 g/2 1/2 oz. lardo or pancetta, cooked**
**100 g/heaped 1 cup Grana Padano cheese, freshly grated, plus extra shavings to garnish**
**1 tablespoon olive oil, for frying**

BATTER

**1 large/US extra-large free-range egg**
**50 g/heaped 1/3 cup Italian 00 flour**
**sea salt, black pepper and nutmeg, to taste**

**Serves 4**

Whisk together all the ingredients for the batter in a bowl until smooth and well combined. Leave to rest for at least 30 minutes, the longer the better.

For the filling, mix the garlic, rosemary and lardo or pancetta together with the grated Grana Padano in a bowl.

Evenly coat the base of a non-stick frying pan/skillet with a little olive oil and set over a medium heat. Pour a small ladleful of batter into the centre of the pan, then gently tilt the pan until a thin layer of batter covers the surface. Cook until the underside of the crêpe is golden. Flip over and cook for a minute or two on the other side.

Spoon a quarter of the filling onto one side of the crêpe, then fold the other side over the top. Remove from the pan and keep warm. Repeat until all the batter and filling has been used to make 4 crêpes. Serve straight away, topped with the Grana Padano shavings.

**190 g/1 1/3 cups Italian 00 flour**
**1/2 teaspoon salt**
**120 ml/1/2 cup water**
**1 tablespoon olive oil for frying**

**TRADITIONAL EGG-FREE VERSION**

Combine all the ingredients in a food processor to make a smooth batter. The batter should have the consistency of double/heavy cream. Add more water if needed, a teaspoon at a time.

# DEEP-FRIED BABY ARTICHOKES & LEMONS WITH MINT & ANCHOVY DRESSING

## CARCIOFI E LIMONI CON ALICI E MENTA

*I grow artichokes in my garden and eagerly await them coming into season in late spring. This is the perfect recipe for young artichokes, which have no fiddly 'choke' to remove. Even though my husband thinks anchovies are evil, he likes this dressing; it adds a delicious piquancy to the dish. I always enjoy sharing* carciofi *with my family in Ravenna.*

**12 small young artichokes**
**2 tablespoons freshly squeezed lemon juice, for acidulating the water**
**2 lemons**
**groundnut oil, for deep frying**

BATTER

**375 g/3 cups Italian 00 flour**
**pinch of sea salt**
**120 ml/½ cup olive oil**
**80 ml/⅓ cup sparkling water**
**1 large/US extra-large egg white**

MINT & ANCHOVY DRESSING

**6 anchovy fillets in olive oil**
**generous handful of fresh mint, leaves only**
**1 tablespoon freshly squeezed lemon juice**
**1 tablespoon red wine vinegar**
**120 ml/½ cup fruity extra virgin olive oil**

*deep-fat fryer or large heavy-based pan suitable for deep-frying*

**Serves 4–6**

Start by making the batter – there will be more than you need but it keeps well in the fridge. Sift the flour into a large bowl, add a pinch of salt and make a well in the centre. Slowly pour in the olive oil, whisking until combined. Gradually add the sparkling water, again whisking until combined. In a separate bowl, whisk the egg white to firm peaks and then gently fold this into the batter. Set aside in the fridge until needed.

To make the dressing, drain and rinse the anchovies, then pat dry with paper towels. Add to a food processor along with the rest of the dressing ingredients and blend to make a vibrant green paste. Taste and add more oil or lemon juice, if liked.

To prepare the artichokes, use a sharp knife to trim and peel the stems. Cut off the tips of the tough outer leaves at the point where their colour becomes dark. Cut the artichokes in half lengthways. (In a young artichoke, there will not be a choke, but for older artichokes, remove any hairy choke as necessary.) Immerse the artichokes in a bowl of water acidulated with a little lemon juice.

Slice the lemons into fairly thin, even rounds – they will be deep-fried so don't make them so thin they will fall apart. Set aside until needed.

When ready to cook, drain the artichokes from their lemon water and pat dry with paper towels.

Heat the groundnut oil in a deep-fat fryer or large heavy-based pan to around 180°C/350°F.

Working in batches of 5 or 6 at a time, dip each artichoke half in the batter, turning to ensure an even coating, then lift out to let any excess batter drain away. Carefully lower the artichokes into the hot oil and deep-fry for about 3–4 minutes until golden. Remove with a slotted spoon and drain on paper towels. Once all the artichokes have been cooked, batter and deep-fry the lemon slices in the same way.

Arrange the hot artichokes and lemon slices on a warm plate and serve with the mint and anchovy dressing for drizzling over or dipping.

# POLENTA WITH BEANS

## CALZAGATTI

*This is a very old recipe prepared in the countryside around the cities of Modena and Reggio Emilia. It is extremely hearty and full of flavour. During my research, I found it most fascinating just how much polenta is enjoyed in this region.*

**1 tablespoon olive oil**
**1 onion, finely chopped**
**100 g/3½ oz. diced pancetta**
**250 g/1⅔ cups fresh or dried borlotti beans, soaked and cooked (see page 49 for instructions)**
**2 x 400-g/14-oz. cans plum tomatoes**
**1 litres/4 cups vegetable broth (see page 40)**
**300 g/2 cups polenta/cornmeal**
**50 g/3½ tablespoons butter**
**100 g/1¼ cups grated Parmigiano Reggiano, plus extra to garnish**
**salt and freshly ground black pepper**
**handful of fresh flat-leaf parsley, roughly chopped, to garnish**

**Serves 4–6**

Heat the oil in a large saucepan over a medium heat and fry the onions and pancetta for 5–10 minutes until golden. Add the cooked and drained borlotti beans, the tomatoes and some salt and pepper and cook gently for 30 minutes. Taste and adjust the seasoning, if needed.

Bring the vegetable broth to the boil in a separate saucepan. Pour the polenta into the pan through your fingers in a fine stream, stirring the polenta into the broth as you are pouring. Cook, stirring continuously, for at least 30 minutes over a medium heat. The polenta is ready when it pulls away from the side of the pan. It should be a very soft consistency. Stir in the butter and cheese. Taste and adjust the seasoning.

Spoon the polenta onto a wooden board and top with the beans. Scatter over an abundance of chopped parsley and more Parmigiano Reggiano to finish.

*Within the historic centre of Modena, the streets are lined with brightly painted buildings. The city is a major centre for food, not least its most famous produce – balsamic vinegar aged in wooden barrels.*

# POTATO & HERB TART

## TORTA DI PATATE ED ERBE

*In the iconic region of Parma, this tart is famous. It is produced with great pride in the* paese *(village) in the Apennine mountain areas of Val Taro and Val Ceno. Spinach is the most popular filling, and I've enjoyed something quite similar in Tuscany, but this version somehow feels like it belongs to the people of Parma. There is so much commotion around this* torta *– enjoyed at family gatherings and picnics, as well as an* antipasti *– and there is an unspoken competitive feeling when the subject is raised. When I was testing the filling for this book, this was the most popular with my family. The potatoes just so happened to be fresh from the garden and so every single ingredient was top quality. During all the seasons, please use the freshest ingredients at their peak to make something so simple, yet so delicious.*

PASTRY

**220 g/1$\frac{3}{4}$ cups Italian 00 flour**
**$\frac{1}{2}$ teaspoon sea salt**
**4 tablespoons olive oil**

FILLING

**1 kg/2$\frac{1}{4}$ lb. cooked potatoes (old potatoes should be baked, then riced or mashed, and new potatoes should be peeled, boiled and sliced**
**125 g/scant 1$\frac{1}{2}$ cups grated Grana Padano**
**1 large onion, finely chopped**
**200 g/7 oz. mascarpone or burrata**
**2 large/US extra-large eggs, beaten (reserving 1 tablespoon of the egg for glazing)**
**1 teaspoon freshly grated nutmeg**
**handful of fresh flat-leaf parsley, chopped**
**handful of fresh rosemary, finely chopped**
**sea salt and freshly ground black pepper**

*28-cm/11-inch loose-bottomed tart pan*

**Serves 6–8**

First, make the pastry. Place the flour and salt in a bowl and use a fork to mix together. Make a well in the flour and add the oil along with 120 ml/$\frac{1}{2}$ cup water. Using the fork, bring the flour into the wet mixture, pulling the dry flour in from the side of the bowl as you mix, to form a rough, shaggy dough. Tip out the dough onto a clean work surface and gently knead until smooth. Let the dough relax in a covered bowl for 30 minutes.

To make the potato filling, combine all of the ingredients in a bowl and season well with salt and pepper.

Preheat the oven to 180°C/160°C fan/350°F/gas 4. Grease and line the tart pan with parchment paper.

Roll out the dough to a circle large enough to line the tart pan with 4 cm/1$\frac{3}{4}$ inches of pastry overhanging the rim of the pan all the way round. Line the pan with the pastry and then fill the pastry case with the potato mixture. Fold the overhanging pastry on top of the filling, pleating and tucking the pastry to make a neat border. The filling will remain visible in the centre. Using a pastry brush, glaze the exposed areas of pastry with the reserved beaten egg. Bake in preheated oven for 35 minutes until the pastry edges are crisp and golden.

Leave on a wire rack to cool, then cut into slices. The torta can be eaten hot, warm or cold as part of an antipasti plate or on a picnic.

**Note:** *Other filling combinations that work well are wilted spinach and ricotta with nutmeg and Grana Padano cheese, and roasted pumpkin and mascarpone with basil and onion.*

# ITALIAN PICKLED VEGETABLES

## LA GIARDINIERA

*Enticingly tangy and crunchy, classic Italian* giardiniera *pickles are easy to make and so handy to keep in the cupboard. I love them as a bright, refreshing side dish to* antipasti.

**1 cauliflower, separated into bite-sized florets**
**2–4 firm carrots, sliced into bite-sized pieces**
**2 firm celery stalks/ribs, sliced into 5-cm/2-inch pieces**
**6 small shallots, peeled and left whole**
**1 red (bell) pepper, sliced into strips or 2.5-cm/1-inch rectangles**
**350 ml/scant 1½ cups white wine vinegar**
**350 ml/scant 1½ cups distilled white vinegar**
**1 tablespoon sea salt**
**1 tablespoon sugar**
**½ teaspoon whole black peppercorns**
**½ teaspoon dried chilli/hot red pepper flakes**
**¼ teaspoon whole cloves**
**¼ teaspoon whole juniper berries**
**1 dried bay leaf**
**3 tablespoons extra-virgin olive oil**
**80 g/3 oz. green olives, stoned/pitted (optional)**

*3 x 550-ml/2½-cup sterilized pickling jars*

**Makes 3 large jars**

Place the prepared vegetables in a large mixing bowl.

Make the pickling liquid. In a saucepan large enough to hold all the vegetables, combine the white wine vinegar and distilled white vinegar with 350 ml/1½ cups water. Stir in the salt and sugar and set the pan over a medium heat. Once the salt and sugar have dissolved, raise the heat to medium-high and bring to the boil. Let the pickling liquid boil for a full 3 minutes.

Briefly hot-pickle the vegetables by turning off the heat and carefully adding the vegetables. Cover and let steep for 1 minute, then use a skimmer or fine-mesh sieve/strainer to scoop the vegetables back into the mixing bowl. Reserve the pickling liquid.

In a small bowl, combine the peppercorns, chilli flakes, cloves and juniper berries. Crumble in the bay leaf with your hands and toss to combine. Divide the spice mix between the three pickling jars.

Pack the vegetables into the jars, adding a mix of the different vegetables to each jar and packing them in as tightly as you can. Pour the pickling liquid over the vegetables, leaving about 2-cm/¾-inch of space at the top.

Spoon 1 tablespoon olive oil into the top of each jar and screw the lids on tightly. Gently turn the jars upside-down and upright again once or twice to encourage the ingredients to mingle. Let the jars sit upright at room temperature for 24 hours.

Store the jars in the fridge. For maximum flavour, leave the *giardiniera* to sit and infuse for a week before using. The pickles can be enjoyed for up to 3 months.

# CARAMELIZED FENNEL, ONION & OLIVE BRUSCHETTA

## BRUSCHETTE DI FINOCCHI, CIPOLLE ED OLIVE

*Fennel has established itself as a deliciously versatile vegetable well beyond the boundaries of its native Italy, where it is eaten raw as a* digestivo. *This is the ideal recipe to convert anyone who remains unconvinced by fennel's charms.*

**15 g/1 tablespoon butter**
**1 tablespoon olive oil**
**2 onions, finely sliced**
**2 fennel bulbs, trimmed, quartered and finely sliced**
**50 ml/scant 1/4 cup white wine**
**8 black olives, stoned/pitted**
**4 large slices open-textured bread, cut 1cm/1/2 inch thick (my ciabatta recipe on page 54 works perfectly)**
**sea salt and freshly ground black pepper**
**fennel fronds, to garnish**

**Serves 4**

Melt the butter and olive oil in a non-stick heavy-based pan. Stir in the onions and fennel and stew slowly over a very low heat for about 45 minutes, stirring from time to time, or until the vegetables are golden brown and tender.

Add the wine and olives and continue cooking until the wine has bubbled away completely. Adjust the seasoning, if needed. Keep the fennel mixture warm while you prepare the bruschetta.

Toast the bread until it is golden brown. Spoon the warm fennel mixture onto the toasted bread and serve at once, topped with a few fennel fronds to finish.

CHAPTER TWO

# SOUP & BREAD
# Zuppa e Pane

*The Torre delle Ghirlandia, the iconic bell tower of the Duomo di Modena, dominates the skyline of the city. In its shadow sits numerous restaurants and trattorias, plus the Mercado Histórico Albinelli, a covered marketplace where you can pick up an array of traditional and local produce.*

# THE PERFECT DUO

SOUP MIGHT NOT IMMEDIATELY spring to mind when considering Italian food, but there are many different types of soups that are much loved across the entire country. They range from plain broths or consommés, sometimes with the addition of pasta or dumplings, to hearty vegetable medleys bolstered further by rice or pasta (the classic minestrone, for instance), and thick vegetable purées. In regions by the sea, fish soups will likely be on offer. All these soups are served as a *primo piatto*, between the appetizer and main course, and should be served instead of a rice or pasta course. Most Italian soups are eaten hot, especially in the northern regions in winter, but some can be served cold.

The essential building block of a decent soup is a good *brodo* (broth); I have given three in this chapter – vegetable, chicken and beef. What elevates any soup is the deep flavour of the broth used to make it interesting, so I urge you to find the time to make your own – your soups will be all the better for it! And soups should always be accompanied by bread, to be eaten alongside and to mop up the last drops left in the bowl. I give you a few typical breads within these pages.

In Emilia-Romagna, we find examples of all the above types of soup. The most famous – which many think is representative of the region – is *passatelli in brodo*, little bread dumplings cooked in broth. Stale bread is made into breadcrumbs, these are mixed with grated cheese, butter and eggs, along with some aromatics, and then the paste is 'passed' through the holes of a special kind of sieve directly into the boiling broth. But, as Elizabeth David writes in *Italian Food*: 'An ordinary metal sieve with large holes, a colander, or even a perforated draining spoon, will do.' The soup itself is a fine example of *cucina povera* (peasant cooking), in which the cook utilizes any inexpensive ingredients that are to hand, demonstrating that particular thrift in which Italians so excel by transforming humble ingredients that might otherwise have been thrown away.

Another soup using bread, again from the *cucina povera* tradition, is *pancotto* (see page 46), which is how it is known in Bologna and all over Emilia-Romagna. In English *pancotto* means 'cooked bread', while elsewhere the soup is called *zuppa di pan*, 'bread soup', or *acquacotta*, 'cooked water'. Bread is soaked in water or milk, then cooked with butter, eggs and cheese, nothing more. It was once a dish for the elderly, children, those who couldn't chew (a lack of teeth would have been quite common at one time), and those who were ill. (Interestingly, the English summer pudding, which uses bread, was once known as 'hydropathic pudding', and was served to those who were ill.) A bread soup would also have been a dish served to everyone on days when meat was proscribed, such as Fridays, according to Catholic tradition.

The third soup to rely on a good *brodo* is my *Minestra del Paradiso (see page 43)*, which is the Emilia-Romagnan version of the Roman *stracciatella* – a broth in which eggs and cheese are cooked. (*Stracciatella* comes from a word meaning 'torn' or 'in rags', which is what the eggs in the soup look like. Oddly, this name is also given to vanilla ice cream with chocolate chips!)

The thicker soups here are ideal for serving as a warming meal in winter. But whatever type of soup you serve, you must also offer some bread. The most famous of the region is *piadina* (see page 57), a thin flatbread, that is traditionally made from lard or olive oil, salt and water, then cooked in a hot pan. I have added yeast to make it more sumptuous, and sparkling rather than still water also lightens the bread. The dough can be rolled into a round, folded and sealed over a filling into a half-moon shape, then cooked in a dry pan. Or, more traditionally, the round can be cooked first and then folded around a delicious filling. These are good served with soups or as *antipasti*. They say a *piadina* varies in thickness, depending on the town: it is thin in Rimini, becoming thicker the further inland you go. However, it must not be too soft or too crisp, it must be just right....

*Piadine* can also be fried, but the best-known fried breads of the region are *crescentine* and *gnocco fritti*. *Crescentine* are also known as *tigelle*, although they seem to be completely different. The idea comes from Modena, and the same dough is used. For *crescentine* (see page 58) the dough is rolled and cut into thin circles, squares or any shape you like, and deep-fried. For *tigelle*, the dough is rolled thicker, and cut into small

round breads, very like English muffins. These are dry-fried in a hot pan until crisp on the outside and soft in the middle. (They can also be cooked in a special hinged, patterned pan, rather like a waffle iron.) Cut in half, they are the perfect vessel for many delicious things, or to accompany soup. *Gnocco fritto* (see page 60) is made from yeasted bread dough, run through the pasta machine, then cut into assorted shapes and deep-fried. A perfect accompaniment to soup, they are also good on a platter of assorted *antipasti*. *Gnocco fritto* in paper cones, either by themselves, or filled with cheese or similar, are one of the most popular street-food snacks in the region.

I have also given you some traditional breads: an olive bread, a ciabatta and a focaccia. More unusual is a speciality bread from Ferrara: *La Coppia Ferrarese* (see page 53) is shaped like a cross with two strips of dough connected in the middle. The shape of the bread was said to be inspired by the curly tresses of the infamous Lucrezia Borgia, who became the Duchess of Ferrara.

# BROTHS

*Making your own broth from scratch can completely transform the flavour of a dish. Using only fresh vegetables, chicken and other meat bones – with no other sinister ingredients added – can mean the differences between a homemade broth and a store-bought stock or a stock cube are night and day; there is no comparison. Like all Italians, I am incredibly frugal, and making my own broth suits this personality trait perfectly. Using up any vegetable scraps to create a flavourful broth can transform a dish from something just acceptable to truly spectacular. I can't emphasize strongly enough what a difference this makes.*

## VEGETABLE BROTH

### BRODO VEGETALE

**1 tablespoon olive oil**
**40 g/1¼ oz. unsalted butter**
**3 garlic cloves, peeled and crushed**
**1 large onion, peeled and coarsely chopped**
**4 leeks, trimmed, washed and coarsely chopped**
**2 carrots, peeled and coarsely chopped**
**2 celery stalks/ribs, coarsely chopped**
**1 fennel bulb, quartered**
**handful of fresh flat-leaf parsley (leaves and stalks)**
**4 fresh bay leaves**
**2 fresh thyme sprigs**
**sea salt and freshly ground black pepper**

**Makes about 1.5 litres/ 2½ pints/6 cups**

Heat the olive oil and butter in a large saucepan or stock pot. Add the garlic and fry gently for 2 minutes. Add the onion, leeks, carrots, celery, fennel and herbs. Cook over a low heat, stirring continuously, until the vegetables are softened, but not browned.

Add 3 litres/5 pints water and bring to the boil. Reduce the heat, cover and simmer for 1 hour. Strain the broth and return to the pan, discarding the vegetables and herbs. Boil rapidly until reduced by half, then season with salt and pepper to taste. Allow to cool.

The broth can be stored in the fridge for up to 3 days, or divided into portions and stored in the freezer for up to 1 month for future use.

# CHICKEN BROTH

## BRODO DI POLLO

**1.4-kg/3-lb. free-range chicken**
**2 onions, peeled and quartered**
**2 celery stalks/ribs, coarsely chopped**
**1 large potato, peeled and quartered**
**4 fresh bay leaves**
**handful of fresh flat-leaf parsley (leaves and stalks)**
**2 fresh thyme sprigs**
**sea salt and freshly ground black pepper**

**Makes about 1.5 litres/ 2½ pints/6 cups**

**Note:** *This broth is ideally made with a good-quality raw chicken. A slightly less flavoursome broth can be made with a raw carcass or cooked carcass left over from a roast.*

Rinse the chicken in cold water, drain well and cut off any visible fat.

Bring 3.4 litres/6 pints water to the boil in a very large saucepan or stock pot over a high heat. Add the chicken to the pan along with the onions, celery, potato and herbs. Bring to the boil and continue to boil rapidly for 5 minutes.

Reduce the heat to low and simmer very slowly, uncovered, for about 2 hours. Skim off any scum from the surface from time to time. Remove the chicken, then strain the broth through a sieve or colander into a bowl and season with salt and pepper to taste. Allow to cool, then chill in the fridge.

Once chilled, remove the solidified fat that has accumulated on the surface of the broth.

The broth can be stored in the fridge for up to 3 days, or divided into portions and stored in the freezer for up to 1 month for future use.

# BEEF BROTH

## BRODO DI MANZO

**1 kg/2¼ lb. beef bones or shin**
**2 large onions, peeled and quartered**
**3 celery stalks/ribs, coarsely chopped**
**1 whole garlic bulb, halved widthways**
**2 carrots, peeled and coarsely chopped**
**2 large tomatoes**
**3 fresh bay leaves**

**Makes about 1.5 litres/ 2½ pints/6 cups**

Preheat the oven to 200°C/180°C fan/400°F/gas 6. Place the beef bones or shin in a roasting pan with the onions and roast in the preheated oven for 30 minutes.

Pour off any fat, then transfer the beef and onions to a very large saucepan. Add 3.4 litres/6 pints water, along with the celery, garlic, carrots, tomatoes and bay leaves. Bring to the boil and continue to boil rapidly for 5 minutes. Reduce to a simmer and continue cooking, half covered, for 2–3 hours.

Remove the bones, then strain the broth through a sieve or colander into a bowl and season with salt and pepper to taste.

The broth can be stored in the fridge for up to 3 days, or divided into portions and stored in the freezer for up to 1 month for future use.

# PASSATELLI IN BROTH

## PASSATELLI IN BRODO

*This is a marvellously delicious way to use up stale breadcrumbs. There are many regional variations on this recipe from the Veneto to the coast of Emilia-Romagna, and to Le Marche even. My grandmother Furiani taught me how to make this dish years ago; I still absolutely love it. It does rely heavily on a hearty* brodo, *so please use the one that I suggest for tortellini (see page 97) or a vegetable broth also works well here (see page 40).*

**1 quantity broth (see page 97)**
**freshly ground black pepper**
**handful of fresh flat-leaf parsley, to garnish**

PASSATELLI
**2 large/US extra-large eggs with golden yolks**
**125 g/1¾ cups stale, dry breadcrumbs, finely crushed**
**130 g/1⅔ cups grated Grana Padano, plus extra to garnish**
**1 teaspoon freshly grated nutmeg**
**1½ tablespoons Italian 00 flour**
**zest of 1 unwaxed lemon**

*potato ricer (or colander)*

**Serves 6**

To make the passatelli dough, combine all of the ingredients in a medium bowl and mix well – it should be quite firm in texture. Cover the bowl and leave the dough to relax for about 25 minutes.

Bring the broth to a gentle simmer in a large saucepan.

Take a piece of the rested dough and press it through a potato ricer directly into the broth – ideally the pieces should be about 7 cm/3 inches long. Keep working as quickly as you can, until you have used all of the dough.

Gently simmer the broth until the passatelli rise to the top and float on the surface. The passatelli are now ready to serve.

Ladle the broth and passatelli into individual bowls and garnish with a good grinding of black pepper, the extra Grana Padano and parsley leaves to finish.

**Note:** *If you don't have a potato ricer, the same effect can be achieved by pushing the dough through the holes of a colander to create the passatelli.*

## HEAVENLY SOUP

### MINESTRA DEL PARADISO

*This recipe is famous all over Emilia. Each household will have their very own variation, from the type of broth used (either vegetable, chicken or meat) to adding parsley or nutmeg and the type and quantity of cheese added, and even sometimes rice.*

**2.5 litres/quarts chicken broth (see page 41)**
**2 large/US extra-large eggs**
**110 g/1¼ cups grated Grana Padano**
**2 teaspoons freshly grated nutmeg**
**handful of chopped fresh flat-leaf parsley**
**sea salt and freshly ground black pepper**

**Serves 4–6**

Heat the broth in a large saucepan over a medium heat.

Beat the eggs in a bowl with the cheese and nutmeg. Pour the beaten eggs into the hot broth and stir well. The eggs will scramble and cook in the broth. Adjust the seasoning, if needed.

Ladle the broth and scrambled eggs into individual bowls and scatter over plenty of parsley to finish.

## POTATO & SAUSAGE SOUP

### ZUPPA DI PATATE E SALSICCIA

*The weather gets very cold in the region, so this is the perfect warming, substantial dish. For the best results, only use ingredients that are in peak condition.*

**1.5 litres/6 cups chicken broth (see page 41)**
**3 potatoes, peeled and sliced**
**1 onion, peeled and finely chopped**
**125 ml/½ cup milk**
**1 tablespoon semolina**
**2 cooked Italian sausages, thinly sliced**
**sea salt and freshly ground black pepper**

TO GARNISH
**handful of fresh flat-leaf parsley, finely chopped**
**freshly grated Grana Padano**

**Serves 6**

Heat the broth in a large saucepan over a medium heat. Add the potatoes and onions and cook for 10–15 minutes, or until the potatoes are soft.

Using a slotted spoon, remove the potatoes and onion from the broth. Pass the potatoes through a potato ricer, or use a masher.

Return the mashed potatoes and the onions to the broth, then add the milk and sprinkle in the semolina. Continue to cook, stirring continuously, for about 10 minutes.

Add the sliced sausages and cook for a further 10 minutes. Season well to taste. Ladle the broth and sausages into individual bowls and scatter over plenty of parsley and Grana Padano to finish.

# BREAD SOUP

## PANCOTTO

*Once considered the food of the poor, when there was only stale bread in the cupboard, this bread soup is now prepared even by those with the most bountiful kitchens. Although this is a dish from Emilia-Romagna, I have enjoyed this soup in other regions too, particularly the Maremma region of Tuscany. It was a hot day, yet I was totally refreshed by the soup.*

**400 g/14 oz. stale country bread, torn into 2.5-cm/1-inch cubes**
**60 g/½ stick/¼ cup unsalted butter**
**100 ml/scant ½ cup olive oil**
**800 ml/3¼ cups broth (any type; see pages 40–41)**
**2 large/US extra-large eggs**
**100 g/1 cup grated Grana Padano**
**sea salt and freshly ground black pepper**
**generous handful of fresh flat-leaf parsley, to garnish**

**Serves 4**

Moisten the cubes of bread with 6 tablespoons water in a bowl for about 1 hour or until the bread is just soft, rather than breaking down completely (how long it takes will depend on how stale the bread is). Squeeze the bread to remove excess water.

Melt half the butter in a large pan with all of the oil. Add the soaked bread with a pinch of salt, then pour in the broth. Bring to the boil and continue boiling for 20 minutes until the bread has completely softened and the soup has thickened.

In a bowl, beat the eggs with the cheese and the remaining butter. Stir a ladleful of the hot broth into the egg mixture, mixing slowly. Add the egg mixture to the pan of soup, mixing thoroughly, until everything is well combined. Ladle the soup into individual bowls and season with plenty of black pepper. Finally, scatter over plenty of finely chopped parsley to garnish.

*The city of Bologna has earned the nickname of La Grassa (The Fat One) due to its reputation for rich cuisine, but it also offers lots of local breads.*

# PASTA & BEANS

## PASTA E FAGIOLI

*I was reluctant to write up this recipe as, up to now, I have been fiercely loyal to my Nonna's* pasta e fagioli. *However, through my research for this book, I discovered that most of the region has a variation on this dish, which is well worth documenting. It is truly magnificent. This soup is pure joy during the fresh bean season from September to October. It also uses the characteristic pasta from Parma. One point of difference is in the meat and the small pieces of Parma ham that are added.*

**300 g/1¾ cups dried borlotti beans (or 1 kg/5¾ cups fresh borlotti beans)**
**3 garlic cloves, finely chopped**
**6 fresh bay leaves**
**150 g/5½ oz. Parma ham, cut into small pieces**
**1 celery stalk/rib, diced**
**1 carrot, diced**
**1 potato, peeled and diced**
**1 onion, finely chopped**
**400-g/14-oz. can plum tomatoes**
**50 g/1¾ oz. Parmigiano Reggiano rind, cubed**
**500 ml/2 cups broth (any type; see pages 40–41) or water**
**125 g/4½ oz. ditalini or quadretti fresh egg pasta**
**good-quality extra virgin olive oil, for drizzling**
**sea salt and freshly ground black pepper**

**Serves 6**

If using dried beans, soak them overnight in a bowl of water with the garlic and 3 of the bay leaves. Drain before using. If using fresh beans, skip the soaking step. Whichever type of bean you are using, add them to a saucepan of water, bring to the boil and cook for 10 minutes to par-cook, then drain before moving on to the rest of the soup.

Heat a large saucepan or stock pot over a medium heat, add the Parma ham and cook until it has taken on some colour. Add the diced vegetables and cook until softened and lightly coloured.

Add the par-cooked beans, plum tomatoes, remaining bay leaves and Parmigiano Reggiano rind to the pan, then pour in the broth or water. Cook over a medium heat for 35 minutes until the beans are tender.

Transfer half the soup to a blender and blitz until smooth (or use a handheld stick/immersion blender. Return all the soup to the pan and add another 500 ml/2 cups water and reheat until boiling. Add the pasta and cook according to the packet instructions until tender.

Season well with plenty of salt and pepper, if needed. Ladle the soup into individual bowls and drizzle over some extra virgin olive oil before serving.

**Note:** *When par-cooking dried borlotti beans, the cooking time can vary hugely depending on how long the packet has been in your cupboard! Very old beans will take much longer to cook. Keep checking and tasting until the beans are perfectly soft and delicious.*

# CHICKEN & ROASTED PEPPER SOUP

## ZUPPA DI POLLO CON PEPPERONI ARROSTITI

*This recipe is based on a soup served at the Ristorante Diana in Bologna. It traditionally uses 'duchese' olive oil and is definitely at its best when you use the highest quality extra virgin oil you can get for finishing the dish.*

**12 red (bell) peppers**
**10 chicken thighs**
**2 tablespoons olive oil**
**1 onion, chopped**
**2 garlic cloves, peeled and crushed**
**1.5 litres/6 cups chicken broth (see page 41), warmed**
**handful of fresh basil leaves, torn**
**handful of fresh mint leaves, roughly chopped**
**2 teaspoons fresh marjoram leaves**
**best-quality extra virgin olive oil, for drizzling**
**sea salt and freshly ground black pepper**

**Serves 6**

Preheat the oven to 200°C/180°C fan/400°F/gas 6.

Roast the peppers in the preheated oven for 25 minutes, then leave to cool. Scrape out the seeds, remove the skins and slice the peppers thinly.

At the same time, cook the chicken thighs. Season them with salt and pepper and roast alongside the peppers for about 20 minutes, or until cooked through. Leave to cool, then discard the chicken skin and bones and finely shred the meat

Heat the oil in a large saucepan or stock pot, add the onion and gently fry until softened and golden.

Add the strips of roasted pepper, shredded chicken, garlic and broth along with the herbs. Simmer for 5 minutes. Adjust the seasoning with salt and pepper, if needed.

Ladle the broth, chicken and peppers into individual warmed bowls and drizzle over the best extra virgin olive oil to finish.

*The striking rooftop skyline and famous towers of Bologna.*

# BREAD ROLLS FROM FERRARA

## LA COPPIA FERRARESE

*This truly historic bread from Ferrara, dating back to 1536, is known as the 'couple' bread because of its distinctive pair of twisted horn shapes.*

**100 g/3½ oz. sourdough starter (use the biga starter from my ciabatta recipe on page 54)**
**500 g/4¼ cups Italian 00 flour, plus extra for dusting**
**40 g/3 tablespoons unsalted butter**
**20 ml/4 teaspoons olive oil**
**1 teaspoon salt**
**1 teaspoon malt extract (can be bought from chemists or online)**
**1 teaspoon dried yeast**

**Makes 8**

**Notes:** *The shaping and forming of this iconic bread can be tricky to master, but it is so worth it if you have a little patience.*

*The temperature in the kitchen is vital here. Cover the dough while you are working on the shapes to avoid the dough drying out.*

Combine all of the ingredients together with 180 ml/¾ cup water in a large bowl, mixing well. Knead on a lightly floured work surface for 10 minutes until the dough is smooth and elastic. Add more flour as needed if the dough is very sticky, or more liquid if it is too dry. The dough should have the texture of Blu Tack/poster putty; not too wet and not too dry. Place the dough in a clean bowl and cover with a damp dish towel. Leave to rise in a warm place, ideally above 20°C/68°F, for 1½ hours.

On a lightly floured surface, knock back the dough by gently pressing your fist into the centre until it deflates. Knead the dough again for 2 minutes or until smooth. Divide the dough into 16 equal pieces (each weighing about 50 g/1¾ oz.).

To form the distinctive horn shapes, roll out each piece of dough into a wide, flat strip about 30 cm/12 inches long. Lay a strip lengthways in front of you and firmly anchor one end by holding the short end closest to you with one hand. Working from the opposite end, using the flat palm and fingers of your other hand, roll up the strip towards you but with every roll work backwards and forwards to stretch and narrow the dough yet to be rolled. The strip should be wider at the start and become narrower as you reach the end – this is what makes the horn shape (which looks like a skinny croissant). Stop rolling when there is about 5 cm/2 inches of the strip left.

Once all the strips have been shaped, place two horns side by side with the free ends facing each other. Fold each free end over onto itself to double it up, then line the horns up with the folded ends touching. Now, squeezing from the outer sides, firmly press the two horns together to make an 'X' shape. Place on a large baking sheet, with plenty of space between them to double in size as they proof, then cover with parchment paper.

When the horns have proofed, preheat the oven to 200°C/180°C fan/400°F/gas 6. Bake the breads for 25 minutes until golden. Leave on a wire rack to cool. Serve the breads in their pairs, ready to be torn apart and shared.

# CIABATTA

## CIABATTA BOLOGNESE

*Ciabatta was given its name because the bread resembles a well-worn slipper. A long proofing time and plenty of liquid produce a very light bread with an open, porous texture. An authentic ciabatta requires a very wet dough that can be tricky to handle and must be started a day in advance. Avoid overworking the dough at all costs, and do not be tempted to add extra flour to make it more manageable. After its long rise, the dough must be handled with a very light touch ('like a baby', as they say in Italy), so that none of the precious air bubbles are knocked out. In Bologna, ciabatta is typically served with burrata and mortadella.*

STARTER

**3 tablespoons tepid milk**
**1/2 teaspoon dried yeast**
**1/4 teaspoon honey or granulated sugar**
**150 g/1 cup strong white bread flour, plus extra for dusting**

DOUGH

**1/2 teaspoon dried yeast**
**4 tablespoons olive oil**
**350 g/2 1/2 cups strong white bread flour, plus extra for dusting**
**1 1/2 teaspoons salt**

**Makes 2 loaves or 4 rolls**

**Note:** *This ciabatta should be eaten within a day. In Italy, bread is kept in linen bags to keep the bread fresh, but most Italians buy bread daily to enjoy it as fresh as possible.*

To make the starter, combine the milk and 150 ml/2/3 cup water in a large bowl, then sprinkle in the yeast. Leave for 5 minutes, then add the honey or sugar and stir to dissolve. Mix in the flour to form a loose batter. Cover the bowl with a tea/dish towel and leave to rise for 12 hours.

To make the dough, sprinkle the yeast into 10 ml/2 teaspoons water in a small bowl. Leave for 5 minutes, then stir to dissolve.

Add the yeasted water and olive oil to the starter and mix well. Mix in the flour and salt to form a wet, sticky dough. Beat steadily with a wooden spoon for 5 minutes; the dough will become springy and start to pull away from the sides of the bowl, but will remain too soft to knead.

Cover the dough with a clean tea/dish towel. Leave to rise for about 3 hours until trebled in size and full of air bubbles.

Generously flour two baking sheets and keep some extra flour nearby to dip your hands in. Do not knock back the dough. Using a dough scraper, divide the dough in half to make two loaves or into quarters to make four rolls while in the bowl. Scoop one half or two quarters of the dough out of the bowl directly onto one of the heavily floured baking sheets.

With floured hands, pull and stretch the dough to form a rectangular loaf, about 30 cm/12 inches long or two rolls each about 15 cm/6 inches long. Dust the loaf and your hands again with more flour. Neaten and plump up the loaf or rolls by running your fingers down each side and gently tucking under the edges of the dough. Repeat with the other half or two quarters of the dough on the second baking sheet.

Leave the loaves or rolls uncovered to proof for about 20 minutes; they will spread out as well as rise.

Preheat the oven to 220°C/200°C fan/425°F/gas 7. Bake the breads for 20 minutes, then lower the oven temperature to 180°C/160°C fan/350°F/gas 4 and bake for a further 10 minutes until risen, golden and hollow-sounding when tapped underneath. Leave to cool on a wire rack.

# ITALIAN FLATBREAD

## PIADINA

*These flatbreads are popular across the entire Emilia-Romagna region, which is not surprising as they are so delicious. In fact, they are now enjoyed the length and breadth of Italy. Even if you are a novice breadmaker, do try these flatbreads as they are relatively simple and quick to bake. I love to eat these piadina folded in half and filled with prosciutto, stracchino cheese, sliced tomatoes and rocket/arugula or basil leaves, but they are equally good with just slices of mortadella.*

**2 teaspoons dried yeast**
**500 g/3½ cups strong white bread flour, plus extra for dusting**
**2 teaspoons salt**
**1 tablespoon olive oil**
**250 ml/1 cup sparkling water**

**Makes 8**

**Note:** *I like to use Mulino Marino 00 flour or Canadian bread flour for best results.*

Sprinkle the yeast into 75 ml/⅓ cup water in a bowl. Leave for 5 minutes, then stir to dissolve.

Mix the flour and salt together in a large bowl. Make a well in the centre of the flour and pour in the yeasted water, the oil and 150 ml/⅔ cup of the sparkling water. Mix in the flour and stir in as much of the remaining sparkling water as needed to form a firm, tender dough. The dough should have the texture of Blu Tack/poster putty; not too wet and not too dry.

Turn out the dough onto a lightly floured surface and knead for about 10 minutes until smooth, shiny and elastic.

Put the dough in a clean bowl, then cover with a damp tea/dish towel. Leave to rise in a warm place, preferably above 20°C/68°F, for about 1 hour until doubled in size.

On a lightly floured surface, knock back the dough by gently pressing your fist into the centre until it deflates. Rest the dough again for 10 minutes.

Divide the dough equally into 8 pieces. On a lightly floured surface, roll out each piece into a 1-cm/½-inch thick round, around 15 cm/6 inches wide. If the dough resists rolling out, leave it to relax for 2 minutes and then continue.

Set a large heavy-based frying pan/skillet over a medium-low heat until very hot (about 8 minutes). Place one of the dough rounds in the hot pan and prick it all over with a fork to prevent air bubbles. Flipping the flatbread frequently to ensure even cooking and avoid scorching, cook until golden brown on both sides – about 5 minutes. Repeat with the remaining dough rounds. Stack the cooked flatbreads on top of each other and cover with a clean towel to keep soft and warm.

# ITALIAN FRIED BREAD

## CRESCENTINE

*Golden and puffy fried breads, these crescentine are deliciously crispy on the outside but soft and fluffy on the inside. A classic bread from the Emilia-Romagna region, they are especially popular in Bologna. Crescentine can be served as an appetizer or with a main dish – either way, feel free to be adventurous when it comes to the toppings.*

**200 g/1½ cups Italian 00 flour or strong white bread flour, plus extra for dusting**
**pinch of salt**
**pinch of bicarbonate soda**
**100 ml/scant ½ cup milk (or plant-based milk)**
**125 ml/½ cup neutral oil (e.g. sunflower or vegetable), for frying**

TOPPINGS
**4 slices of best-quality mortadella or Parma ham**
**1–2 balls of mozzarella**
**handful of fresh basil, torn**
**handful of wild rocket/arugula**
**sea salt and freshly ground black pepper**
**best-quality extra virgin olive oil, to garnish**

**Makes 6**

Mix the flour, salt and bicarbonate of soda together in a bowl. Make a well in the centre of the flour and gradually pour in the milk, little by little, and mix in the flour. I find it easiest to do this with a fork. The dough should be damp, not wet.

Turn out the dough onto a lightly floured surface and gently knead for 5 minutes until smooth and like a piece of marble.

Divide the dough equally into 6 pieces, then roll out each piece into a very thin round, around 18 cm/7 inches wide.

Heat the oil in a large heavy-based frying pan/skillet. One at a time, fry the dough rounds in the hot oil until crisp and golden brown. Repeat with the remaining dough rounds. Transfer the cooked breads to paper towels to absorb any excess oil, then cover to keep warm.

Top with your choice of mortadella or Parma ham, mozzarella, basil and rocket. Season to taste and drizzle with the best-quality extra virgin olive oil.

# ITALIAN FRIED DOUGH

## GNOCCO FRITTO

Gnocco fritto *are popular throughout Emilia-Romagna, whether enjoyed as a street food or as part of a* tagliere misto *(**see page 14**). Before being fried, the dough can be made into any shape you like – I have seen some quite dramatic shapes at different restaurants.*

**200 g/1½ cups Italian 00 flour, plus extra for dusting**
**1 teaspoon salt**
**½ teaspoon sugar**
**½ teaspoon dried yeast**
**35 ml/2 tablespoons olive oil**
**100 ml/scant ½ cup sparkling water**
**1 litre/4 cups groundnut oil, for frying**
**semolina, for sprinkling**

**Makes many! (enough to feed a family of 16)**

Combine the flour, salt, sugar and yeast in a bowl using a fork. Make a well in the centre of the flour, add the oil and sparkling water and continue to mix in the bowl with vigour until a smooth dough is formed.

Turn out the dough onto a lightly floured surface and knead for at least 6–8 minutes until smooth and stretchy. Return the dough to a clean bowl, then cover with a damp cloth. Leave to rise in a warm place, preferably above 20°C/68°F, for about 1½ hours until doubled in size.

Knock back the dough to deflate it, then knead lightly. Divide the dough equally into 4 pieces. Roll one piece of the dough through a pasta machine, starting at the widest setting and moving through to the second to last. For a gathering of up to 4 people, one piece of the dough will be enough, so roll out as much dough as the occasion requires.

Heat the oil in a deep saucepan to 180°C/350°F.

Cut the dough into small triangles, squares or diamonds. Working in small batches to avoid overcrowding the pan, fry the gnocco in the hot oil until puffed and golden on each side – this will be quick. Transfer the cooked gnocco to paper towels to absorb any excess oil. Sprinkle with semolina as desired and serve hot or warm as part of a *tagliere misto*.

**Note:** *For a healthier option, the gnocco can be baked in a hot oven at 180°C/160°C fan/ 350°F/ gas 4 on a baking sheet lined with parchment paper for 12–15 minutes until golden.*

# OLIVE BREAD WITH ONION FILLING

## PANE CON CIPOLLA E OLIVE

*Enjoyed at Paolo Atti & Figli Panificio, an iconic bakery in Bologna – delicious!*

DOUGH

**15 g/½ oz. fresh yeast**

**275 ml/9½ fl oz. warm water, at blood temperature**

**500 g/3½ cups strong white bread flour**

**1 teaspoon salt**

**2 tablespoons olive oil, plus extra for oiling**

**70 g/2½ oz. olives (the best quality you can get), drained, stoned/pitted and sliced**

FILLING

**1 tablespoon olive oil**

**2 red onions, peeled and chopped**

**2 fresh bay leaves**

**1 fresh rosemary sprig, leaves picked from the stalks**

**2 tablespoons red wine vinegar**

**55 g/¼ cup soft brown sugar**

TO FINISH

**olive oil**

**sea salt**

**handful of fresh rosemary leaves**

**Serves 6–8**

Dissolve the yeast in the warm water in a small bowl.

Sift the flour directly onto a work surface and make a well in the centre. Add the salt and olive oil. Gradually add the yeasted water and incorporate the flour to form a dough. Knead the dough by hand for 10–15 minutes until smooth and elastic. Add the olives to the dough and continue kneading until they are evenly distributed.

Lightly oil a bowl large enough to allow the dough to double in size. Put the dough in the bowl and cover with a damp cloth. Leave to rise in a warm place for 40 minutes.

Meanwhile, make the onion filling. Heat the olive oil in a pan and add the onions, bay leaves and rosemary. Brown the onions well over a low-medium heat, stirring regularly to prevent them sticking. Add the vinegar and stir well to deglaze the pan. Finally, add the sugar and cook over a low heat for 30 minutes. The onion mixture should be thick, shiny and deep red. Cool completely. (This filling can be made in advance and kept in the fridge for a couple of days.)

Knock back the dough, then divide it in half and shape each piece into a ball. Leave to relax for 10 minutes.

Roll out each ball of dough into a long flat oval shape. Place half the onion mixture and a few extra rosemary leaves slightly off-centre on one half of the dough, leaving a clear border around the edge. Fold the empty half of the dough over to cover the filling and pinch the edges together to make a sealed parcel. Lightly brush the exposed dough with olive oil and sprinkle over some salt and rosemary leaves. Place the filled parcels on a lightly greased baking tray and leave to proof in a warm place for 40 minutes.

Preheat the oven to 200°C/180°C fan/400°F/gas 6. Bake the breads for 20 minutes, or until golden brown and hollow-sounding when tapped underneath. Remove from the oven, brush with more olive oil and leave to cool on a wire rack. Cut the breads into slices before serving.

# OLIVE FOCACCIA

## FOCACCIA ALLE OLIVE

*Each region has their own variation on focaccia, the 'hearth bread' – some are fairly flat while others are deeper. Adding wine lends a lightness to the dough and good-quality olives will always make a difference to the depth of flavour. I've tried so many different kinds of focaccia, but this is absolutely the best version in my opinion.*

**2 teaspoons dried yeast**
**500 g/3½ cups strong white bread flour, plus extra for dusting**
**1½ teaspoons salt**
**75 ml/⅓ cup olive oil, plus extra to finish**
**75 ml/⅓ cup dry white wine**
**200g/7 oz. black olives, drained, stoned/pitted and coarsely chopped**
**2 tablespoons fresh thyme leaves**
**1 tablespoon chopped fresh oregano (or 3 teaspoons dried oregano)**

**Serves 8–10**

**Variation:** Focaccia alla Salvia *(Focaccia with Sage)*
*Follow the instructions for the dough up to step 3. Add 20 chopped fresh sage leaves to the 'sponge' along with the olive oil and white wine. Mix in the flour and stir in the water, then continue as directed in the remaining steps, replacing the oregano, olives and thyme with 1½ teaspoons coarse salt, 2 tablespoons olive oil and 10 fresh sage leaves. Preheat the oven and bake as directed.*

Sprinkle the yeast into 100 ml/scant ½ cup water in a bowl. Leave for 5 minutes, then stir to dissolve.

Mix the flour and salt together in a large bowl. Make a well in the centre of the flour and pour in the yeasted water. Use a wooden spoon to draw enough of the flour into the yeasted water to form a soft paste. Cover the bowl with a tea/dish towel, then leave to 'sponge' for about 20 minutes until frothy and risen.

Pour the olive oil and wine into the well, then mix in the rest of the flour. Stir in up to 75 ml/⅓ cup water to form a soft, sticky dough.

Turn out the dough onto a lightly floured surface. Knead for about 10 minutes until smooth and elastic. Work 125 g/4½ oz. of the olives and 1 tablespoon of the thyme leaves into the dough towards the end of kneading.

Put the dough in an oiled bowl and cover with a tea towel. Leave to rise for about 1½–2 hours until doubled in size.

Knock back the dough to deflate it and chafe for 5 minutes, then leave to rest for 10 minutes.

On a lightly floured surface, roll out the dough into a 1-cm/½-inch thick round, about 24 cm/9½ inches wide. Place on an oiled baking sheet, cover with a tea towel and leave to proof for about 1 hour until doubled in size.

Preheat the oven to 200°C/180°C fan/400°F/gas 6.

Gently press your fingertips into the surface of the dough to form dimples about 1 cm/½ inch deep. Scatter over the remaining olives, thyme and the oregano.

Bake the bread in the preheated oven for 30 minutes until golden brown and hollow-sounding when tapped underneath. Immediately drizzle with more olive oil, then leave to cool on a wire rack.

CHAPTER THREE

# PASTA, GNOCCHI & RICE

## Pasta, Gnocci e Riso

*An iconic symbol of the city and site of pilgrimage, the Santuario Madonna di San Luca overlooks the streets of Bologna.*

# PASTA REIGNS SUPREME

AS THE SAYING GOES, *in Italia si mangia molta pasta* – 'in Italy we eat a lot of pasta' – and this is particularly true in Emilia-Romagna. There are many foodstuffs that have made the region famous, but the fresh egg pasta dishes must surely outstrip them all. Although, of course, these pastas quite often rely on those other famous foodstuffs for their success. Pasta truly does reign supreme in Emilia-Romagna, with the capital, Bologna, regarded country-wide as its natural home. Everyone here is in agreement about the foremost importance of pasta.

There are basically two types of pasta: dried and fresh. Many of the pastas used in Emilia-Romagna (as across the rest of Italy) are dried. Most dried pastas are factory made. Barilla, the family run pasta manufacturer, is based in Parma. However, the dough used for the region's famous filled pastas – tortellini, tortelloni, tortelli, cappelletti, cappellacci, anolini and ravioli – is always freshly made either at home or in a deli or restaurant by a *sfoglino* (fresh pasta maker). *Fare la sfoglia*, 'to make traditional pasta dough', is considered to be an art form, and is a respected profession.

These pastas are made from soft wheat flour, rather than durum or hard wheat flour, as in the south. (I use Italian 00 flour, preferring the brand Mulino Marino, available in good delis, supermarkets and online.) This pasta dough is very malleable and can be used for shapes other than filled: for long spaghetti, tagliatelle and lasagne, and for short farfalle, triglie, fusilli and garganelli. It is also the basis for the famous green lasagne sheets that are used in one of the best-known of Bologna's dishes, *lasagne verdi alla Bolognese* (see page 86). Spinach is added to the basic pasta recipe in place of one of the eggs to keep the proportions even.

All of these pastas are available dried, and, to address one of the most repeated questions about pasta, neither fresh nor dried is inherently superior to the other. It is just that they are different, the main difference being in texture. Fresh pasta is meant to be soft in the mouth, whereas dried pasta is cooked until it can, famously, be classified as *al dente* ('to the tooth') when there is still a little resistance left.

Tortellini are the most famous pasta shapes of Bologna. Traditionally filled with pork, prosciutto, mortadella and Parmigiano Reggiano, tortellini are cooked and served in a flavourful broth, often made with capon. This is a popular dish at celebratory times, including Christmas and Easter, and Italians even use a phrase *mangiamo tortellini* ('we eat tortellini') to mean 'let's celebrate!' It is claimed that the ring shape of tortellini resembles the perfect navel of Venus, the goddess of love, which was recreated in pasta by an innkeeper after spying on her through a keyhole.

Tortelli can be found all over Emilia-Romagna. They vary in shape, but are usually square, rectangular or semi-circular. Most frequently stuffed with herbs, here I have borrowed the roast pumpkin filling associated with the cappellacci from Ferrara, while the cappellacci I give here, with their bishop's mitre shape, are stuffed with cheese to be served, as so many pastas are, with the famous Bolognese ragù. To make ragù, you must use a combination of beef or pork, or sometimes also veal, and the sauce must be cooked for a long time. Please remember that Emilians most certainly don't serve ragù with spaghetti – the correct pasta is tagliatelle. Interestingly, the shape of tagliatelle is said to have been inspired by Lucrezia Borgia's long wavy hair: that hair must have been quite something as it is also connected to the traditional bread of Ferrara (see page 53).

Gramigne, short pasta squiggles, are found in the region – with a sausage sauce like the one I offer here with tagliatelle – and are usually available dried, as are garganelli, pointed tubes, although I give you a recipe here for making them at home. There is even a pasta pie, a popular dish in Ferrara, the *pasticcio ferrarese*, filled with pasta, ragù, white sauce and mushrooms, encased in shortcrust pastry. And, of course, pasta can also be sweet (see page 179).

I hope that you try making pasta at home. Rolling out the dough by hand or with a pasta machine gives me such pleasure. The physical exertion is considered good for you: Italians say it pumps blood from the heart to the fingertips, or vice versa. It may be a generational thing, however: my daughter Antonia happily and adeptly uses our pasta machine. And remember, whenever you have some pasta dough left over, never waste it. Roll it out and cut it into tiny pieces, like quadretti, to dry for later or to use straight away.

The vital final ingredient in any pasta dish – with the exception of those containing fish, according to purists – is Parmigiano Reggiano, grated to sprinkle on top. This hard cheese is made from the evening milk of cows in the provinces of Parma and Reggio Emilia. After curdling, the cheese is wrapped in linen, put into special round moulds and left to mature in a controlled environment for at least 12 months, but up to 40 months. The cheese is checked regularly for cracks, then turned so that it dries and hardens evenly. The 'king of cheese', Parmigiano is full of umami flavour and is so hard that it has to be cut into pieces with a special knife. When I got married over 20 years ago, we had a whole Parmigiano Reggiano on offer, with special knives for guests to use!

Another hard cheese, Grana Padano (the *grana* meaning 'grainy' and *Padano* meaning 'from the Po Valley') is also produced in Emilia-Romagna. It can be grated for use in filled pastas or for sprinkling over the top. Don't forget, never throw away the rind of a hard Italian cheese: add it to soups, sauces and stews where its flavour will permeate and enhance the dish. Just remember to remove the rind before serving.

*This unlikely pairing of pasta and prosciutto dates back to 1901 when two small tribes in Emilia-Romagna held a combined festival to celebrate these two regional foodstuffs.*

# TAGLIATELLE WITH PROSCIUTTO

## TAGLIATELLE CON PROSCIUTTO

FRESH EGG PASTA

**200 g/1½ cups Italian 00 flour**
**2 large/US extra-large free-range eggs with golden yolks**
**semolina, for sprinkling**

SAUCE

**1 shallot, finely diced**
**60 g/¼ cup/½ stick unsalted butter**
**120 g/4½ oz. prosciutto, ideally cut into pieces thicker than prepacked slices**
**30ml/2 tablespoons white wine**
**6 ripe tomatoes, peeled, deseeded and roughly chopped**
**sea salt and freshly ground black pepper**

TO GARNISH

**generous handful of fresh flat-leaf parsley**
**50 g/⅔ cup grated Parmigiano Reggiano**

**Serves 4–6**

First, make the pasta dough. Tip the flour onto a clean surface (ideally wood), then make a well in the centre of the flour. Crack the eggs into the well. Using a fork, break up the eggs so the whites and yolks are combined. Now, using the fork, mix in the flour. At first, it might look a bit like scrambled eggs but keep whisking with the fork until the eggs and flour are well mixed.

Knead the dough with the heel of your hand until it is smooth and stretchy, adding semolina if necessary. The dough should be beautifully smooth and shiny. Wrap the dough in cling film/plastic wrap and leave to relax. How long this take will depend on the temperature of your kitchen – just 5 minutes in a cold kitchen, for 10–15 minutes in the fridge in a warm kitchen.

Meanwhile, start the sauce. In a saucepan, gently fry the shallot in the butter for about 5 minutes until lightly coloured. Add the prosciutto and fry for a further 3 minutes. Pour in the wine and cook until evaporated. Add the tomatoes, season with salt and pepper and cook for 6 minutes until all the flavours have combined.

Divide the pasta dough in half, keeping one piece covered. Run first piece of dough through a pasta machine, starting with the widest setting. After passing it through the three widest settings, laminate the dough by folding it into three (like a letter), then turn the dough through 90 degrees so that the folded ends become the new side edges. Run the dough through the pasta machine again, working through the first three settings.

Fold the dough in half and, starting again with the widest setting, run the dough through the pasta machine but this time leading with the folded edge. Run the dough through the machine again on the second setting. Lay the length of dough onto semolina and leave to dry. Repeat the process with the other piece of dough.

When the dough has dried a little, cut both lengths in half then use a pasta cutter to make into 2-cm/¾-inch wide tagliatelle.

To cook the pasta, bring a large saucepan of salted water to the boil. Add the tagliatelle and cook for 4–6 minutes until al dente. Using tongs, transfer the cooked pasta to the pan with the sauce. Scatter in the parsley and mix well. Serve in warm bowls sprinkled with grated Parmigiano Reggiano.

# CHEESE CAPPELLACCI WITH BOLOGNESE SAUCE

## CAPPELLACCI ALLA BOLOGNESE

*In Emilia-Romagna it is traditional to serve these cappellacci with a rich meat sauce but, if you prefer, you can serve them with a simple tomato sauce or just melted butter and sage for a lighter version.*

**½ quantity fresh egg pasta dough (see page 73)**
**flour, for dusting**
**2 litres/8 cups beef broth (see page 41)**
**½ quantity Bolognese Sauce (see page 86), reheated**
**freshly shaved Parmigiano Reggiano, to serve**

FILLING
**250 g/9 oz. ricotta**
**85 g/3 oz. Taleggio, rind removed and diced very small**
**4 tablespoons freshly grated Parmigiano Reggiano**
**1 small egg**
**½ teaspoon freshly grated nutmeg**
**sea salt and freshly ground black pepper**

*6-7.5-cm/2½-3-inch square ravioli cutter (optional)*

**Serves 6–8 generously**

First, make the filling. Put the ricotta, Taleggio and grated Parmigiano Reggiano in a bowl and mash together with a fork. Add the egg and freshly grated nutmeg, then season with salt and pepper to taste. Stir well to mix.

Using a pasta machine, roll out one-quarter of the pasta dough into a 90–100-cm/36–40-inch long strip. Cut the strip in half with a sharp knife into two 45–50-cm/18–20-inch long strips. Using a sharp knife or fluted ravioli cutter, cut 6 or 7 squares from one of the pasta strips.

Using a teaspoon, put a mound of filling in the centre of each square. Brush a little water around the edge of each square, then fold the square diagonally in half over the filling to make a triangular shape. Press to seal. Wrap the triangle around one of your index fingers, bringing the bottom two corners together. Pinch the ends together to seal, then press with your fingertips around the top edge of the filling to make an indentation so that the 'hat' looks like a bishop's mitre. Put the cappellacci on a lightly floured clean tea/dish towel, sprinkle with more flour and leave to dry. Repeat the process with the remaining dough to make 48–56 cappellacci in total.

Bring the broth to the boil in a large saucepan. Drop the cappellacci into the pan, bring the broth back to the boil, reduce the heat and cook at a gentle simmer for 4–5 minutes.

Drain the cappellacci (the broth will have lost some flavour but could still be saved and used for making soup) and divide them equally between 6–8 warmed bowls. Spoon the hot Bolognese sauce over the cappellacci and shave over the Parmigiano to serve.

**Note:** *I often like to garnish with fresh basil leaves if I have any to hand.*

# SAUSAGE & FENNEL TAGLIATELLE

## TAGLIATELLE AL RAGÙ DI SALSICCIA

*To an Italian, fennel seeds are regarded as an ingredient that aids digestion. Crushing the seeds helps to develop their flavour and adds depth to a dish. I love the combination of sausage and fennel seeds, although they can be left out if you are not a fan of their aniseed flavour. This ragù is a celebration of sausages, a hugely important foodstuff for the Bolognese people.*

**1 tablespoon olive oil**
**400 g/14 oz. rustic Italian pork sausages, skins removed**
**1 onion, finely chopped**
**2 teaspoons fennel seeds**
**1 teaspoon dried chilli flakes/ hot red pepper flakes**
**5 or 6 large fresh sage leaves**
**1 fresh rosemary sprig**
**2 large garlic cloves, thinly sliced**
**150 ml/scant 2/3 cup dry white wine**
**100 ml/scant 1/2 cup single/ light cream**
**150 ml/scant 2/3 cup chicken broth (see page 41)**
**1 quantity fresh taglitelle (see page 73)**
**sea salt and freshly ground black pepper**
**50 g/1/2 cup grated Grana Padano, to serve**

**Serves 4–6**

Heat half the oil in a large pan over a medium heat. Add the sausages and cook for 8 minutes, breaking up the meat with a wooden spoon as it cooks and stirring regularly.

Add the onion, fennel seeds, chilli flakes, sage and rosemary and cook for 5–10 minutes. Add the garlic and wine and cook for a few more minutes until the wine has reduced by half. Add the cream and chicken broth and simmer for 20 minutes. Adjust the seasoning to taste.

To cook the pasta, bring a saucepan of salted water to the boil. Add the tagliatelle and cook for 4–6 minutes until al dente.

Using tongs, transfer the cooked pasta to the pan with the sausage ragù and mix well. Serve in warm bowls sprinkled with grated Grana Padano.

*The River Trebbia flows through the city of Bobbia in the province of Piacenza. Crossed by an historic bridge, the river would once have been fished daily to provide food for the locals.*

# TAGLIATELLE WITH TRUFFLE

## TAGLIATELLE AL TARTUFO

*It was a revelation to discover white truffles in Bologna, but there they were. I was told rather secretively to get truffles with someone who gathers them in the hills with a truffle hunting dog.*

*In the restaurant Mamma Maria in Bologna, this treatment is the best way to make and serve truffles with tagliatelle, and I happen to agree.*

**100 g/$^1/_2$ cup/1 stick unsalted butter**
**75 g/$^3/_4$ cup grated Parmiggano Reggiano cheese, plus extra to serve**
**100 ml/scant $^1/_2$ cup hot chicken broth (see page 41)**
**100 g/3$^1/_2$ oz. white truffle (ideally fresh truffle, but truffle paste is an acceptable alternative. I like the brand Urbani)**
**1 quantity fresh tagliatelle (see page 73)**
**sea salt and freshly ground black pepper**

**Serves 4–6**

Melt the butter in a saucepan. Add the grated cheese and pour in the hot broth. Season generously with salt and plenty of black pepper, then shave in the fresh white truffle, reserving a little for the garnish, or stir in the truffle paste.

To cook the pasta, bring a large saucepan of salted water to the boil. Add the tagliatelle and cook for 4–6 minutes until al dente.

Using tongs, transfer the cooked pasta to the pan with the sauce and mix well. Serve in warm bowls sprinkled with some extra grated Parmigiano and the remaining truffle shaved over the top.

*The pasta dishes of the Emilia-Romagna region are extremely simple, but they rely on the freshest ingredients. One of my visits to Bologna happily coincided with the summer pea season and so I can categorically confirm that it is always best to use good-quality seasonal vegetables.*

# SPAGHETTI WITH PEAS

## PASTA CON I PISELLI

**25 g/1 1/2 tablespoons unsalted butter**
**1 small onion, finely chopped**
**1 celery stalk/rib, finely chopped**
**50 g/1 3/4 oz. pancetta, finely chopped**
**750 g/1 lb. 10 oz. podded fresh peas**
**100 g/3 1/2 oz. prosciutto, sliced and each slice cut into 4 pieces**
**100 ml/scant 1/2 cup broth (any type; see pages 40–41)**
**400 g/14 oz. dried spaghetti**
**grated Parmigiano Reggiano, to serve**
**handful of fresh parsley, finely chopped**
**sea salt and freshly ground black pepper**

**Serves 4**

To make the sauce, melt the butter in a pan over a medium heat. Add the onion, celery and pancetta, then cook until the onion is softened and golden. Stir in the peas and prosciutto, then pour in the broth.

Lower the heat and cover the pan with a lid. Continue cooking until the peas are tender, checking regularly and adding more broth as needed. Season with plenty of salt and pepper.

Meanwhile, cook the spaghetti in a saucepan of boiling salted water according to the instructions on the packet. Drain the spaghetti and return it to the pan.

Tip the sauce into the pan with the spaghetti, then toss to mix well. Adjust the seasoning with more salt and pepper as needed.

Serve in warm bowls sprinkled with some grated Parmigiano and finely chopped parsley over the top to finish.

# GARGANELLI WITH SEASONAL VEGETABLES

## GARGANELLI CON VERDURE DI STAGIONE

*The large quill shape of this pasta is classic of the region and holds sauce beautifully.*

**3 tablespoons olive oil**
**2 carrots, diced**
**1 celery stalk/rib, diced**
**1 garlic clove, peeled and crushed**
**1 small red onion, chopped**
**2 small courgettes/zucchini, diced**
**115 g/3/4 cup freshly podded peas**
**2 ripe tomatoes, diced**
**1 teaspoon fresh thyme leaves**
**handful of fresh basil leaves, torn**
**handful of chopped fresh flat-leaf parsley**
**350 g/12 oz. fresh or dried garganelli (see page 82)**
**2 tablespoons double/heavy cream**
**sea salt and freshly ground black pepper**
**grated Parmigiano Reggiano, to serve**

**Serves 4**

Heat the oil in a saucepan over a low heat. Add the carrots, celery, garlic, onion, courgettes and peas and gently cook, stirring frequently, for 10 minutes until tender.

Add the tomatoes, cover the saucepan with a lid and cook over a low heat for about 6 minutes or until the tomatoes start to break down. Add the herbs and season with salt and pepper to taste.

Meanwhile, cook the pasta in a large pan of boiling salted water until al dente. For fresh garganelli, follow the instructions on page 85; for dried garganelli, cook according to the instructions on the packet. Drain the cooked garganelli and return it to the pan.

Tip the sauce into the pan with the garganelli, then toss to mix well. Add the cream and grated Parmigiano Reggiano to taste. Adjust the seasoning with more salt and pepper as needed. Serve in warm bowls.

# TONINA'S GARGANELLI PASTA

## GARGANELLI ALLA ZINGARA

*This is Tonina's recipe, a fabulously generous cook who I met on my travels around the region. She was eager for me to share her recipe for everyone to enjoy.*

**1 quantity fresh egg pasta dough (see page 73)**
**semolina, for sprinkling**

SAUCE
**200 g/7 oz. pancetta**
**1 onion, finely chopped**
**150 g/5½ oz. sliced mushrooms**
**50 g/1¾ oz. stoned/pitted green olives**
**400 g/14 oz. passata (sieved tomatoes)**
**tiny pinch of peperoncino or cayenne pepper**
**sea salt**
**grated Parmigiano Reggiano, to serve**

*cavatelli or gnocchi paddle and rod*

**Serves 4–6**

Roll out the dough by hand or using a pasta machine into a *sfoglia* (an uncut fresh pasta sheet) and cut it into 5-cm/2-inch squares, sprinkling with semolina if needed.

Lay one pasta square on the paddle at an angle to make a diamond shape. Place the rod just inside the corner of the corner closest to you, flip the corner over the rod and tuck it under at the front (as shown on page 84). Place your hands on each end of the rod and roll the pasta along the paddle to create a tube, making sure it is properly sealed by pressing down when the tip furthest from you is underneath. It is not difficult to do, but it can be time consuming.

Chop the pancetta into cubes, then gently fry in a shallow pan to release some of its fat. Add the onion and fry for 5 minutes until softened. Add the mushrooms, olives, passata and peperoncino or cayenne pepper, then simmer for 20 minutes. Taste the sauce after 10 minutes to see if it needs any salt – this will depend on the saltiness of your olives.

To cook the pasta, bring a large saucepan of salted water to the boil. Add the garganelli, bring the water back to the boil and cook them for 3–5 minutes. How long they take to cook will depend on how thick you have rolled the pasta dough. Check a few garganelli for doneness – they should still be a bit chewy. Drain.

Tip the sauce into the pan with the garganelli, then toss to mix well. Serve in warm bowls sprinkled with grated Parmigiano, if using.

# GARGANELLI WITH ASPARAGUS & CREAM

## GARGANELLI CON ASPARAGI E PANNA

*A speciality of Romagna, garganelli are made from squares of pasta rolled into grooved quill shapes. Traditionally, they were made on pieces of a weaving loom, known as a* pettine, *or 'comb', but nowadays a special paddle and rod are used.*

**bunch of young asparagus (about 250–350 g/9–12½ oz.)**
**350 g/12½ oz. fresh or dried garganelli (see page 82)**
**25 g/1 oz. unsalted butter**
**200 ml/generous ¾ cup double/heavy cream**
**2 tablespoons dry white wine**
**85–115 g/1–1¼ cups grated Parmigiano Reggiano**
**2 tablespoons chopped mixed fresh herbs, such as basil, flat-leaf parsley, marjoram and oregano**
**sea salt and freshly ground black pepper**

**Serves 4**

Trim the woody ends from the asparagus spears. Cut the spears at an angle into pieces that are roughly the same length and shape as the garganelli.

Reserving the tips, blanch the asparagus pieces in a saucepan of boiling salted water for 2 minutes, adding the tips for the second minute only. Immediately drain the asparagus spears and tips, then rinse in cold water and set aside.

To cook the pasta, bring a large saucepan of salted water to the boil. Add the garganelli, bring the water back to the boil and cook them for 3–5 minutes. How long they take to cook will depend on how thick you have rolled the pasta dough. Check a few garganelli for doneness – they should still be a bit chewy. If you are using dried garganelli, cook according to the packet instructions.

Meanwhile, put the butter and cream in a separate saucepan. Add some salt and pepper and bring to the boil. Simmer for a few minutes until the cream reduces slightly and thickens. Add the asparagus, wine and about half the grated Parmigiano Reggiano. Taste and adjust the seasoning if needed. Keep over a low heat.

Drain the cooked pasta and tip it into a warm serving bowl. Pour over the sauce, sprinkle with the chopped herbs and toss well. Serve topped with the remaining grated Parmigiano.

# LASAGNE BOLOGNESE

## LASAGNE VERDI ALLA BOLOGNESE

SPINACH PASTA

**150 g/3 cups spinach, cooked and squeezed dry**
**300 g/10½ oz. semolina, plus extra for dusting**

BOLOGNESE SAUCE

**50 g/3½ tablespoons unsalted butter**
**1 onion, finely chopped**
**1 celery stick/rib, finely chopped**
**1 carrot, finely chopped**
**500 g/1 lb. 2 oz. minced/ground pork (10% fat)**
**500 g/1 lb. 2 oz. minced/ground beef (10% fat)**
**3 fat garlic cloves, finely sliced**
**1½ teaspoons ground cinnamon**
**3 fresh bay leaves, torn**
**400-g/14-oz. can whole plum tomatoes**
**3 tablespoons tomato purée/paste**
**3 tablespoons whole/full-fat milk**
**sea salt and freshly ground back pepper**
**fresh basil leaves, for layering**

BÉCHAMEL SAUCE

**30 g/2 tablespoons unsalted butter**
**30 g/2 tablespoons Italian 00 flour**
**450 ml/1¾ cups whole/full-fat milk, hot**
**2 teaspoons freshly grated nutmeg**
**125 g/1½ cups freshly grated Grana Padano, plus extra to serve**

*30-cm/12-inch square baking dish*

**Serves 6**

First, make the spinach pasta dough. Blend the cooked spinach and semolina in a food processor to make a firm dough. Wrap the dough in cling film/plastic wrap and transfer to the fridge to rest.

Next, make the Bolognese. Melt the butter in a large saucepan over a medium heat. Add the onion, celery and carrot and cook for 5–10 minutes until golden. Add both meats, increase the heat to high and cook, breaking up any clumps with a wooden spoon, until browned. Add the garlic, cinnamon, bay leaves, plum tomatoes and tomato purée. Season with plenty of black pepper and add 1.5 litres/ 6 cups water. Simmer over a low heat for 4 hours, adding more seasoning periodically and topping up the liquid with up to 60 ml/¼ cup water if needed. Add the milk halfway through the cooking time.

To make the béchamel sauce, melt the butter in a separate pan over a low heat. Add the flour, stirring rapidly with a wooden spoon and cook for 1 minute to cook out the flour. While stirring continuously, gradually add half the hot milk making sure there are no lumps. Slowly add the remaining milk, season with salt, pepper and nutmeg, then continue to cook until the sauce is glossy. Add the cheese, stir until melted, then take the pan off the heat. Cover and set aside.

While the Bolognese is cooking, make the lasagne sheets. On a surface lightly dusted with semolina, roll out half the pasta dough with a rolling pin to a very thin sheet – so thin that it looks likes a sheet of paper and if you blow on it, the pasta lifts from the work surface. Leave the pasta to dry out a little. Once dried, cut the pasta sheet into enough wide strips to make three layers within the lasagne dish – I recommend making them roughly 10 x 6 cm/4 x 2½ inches.

Bring a large saucepan of salted water to a rolling boil. Working two at a time, cook the pasta strips for 2 minutes. Using a slotted spoon, lift the par-cooked pasta strips out of the pan and lay them out on a clean dry tea/dish towel to drain. Once all the pasta strips have been par-cooked, assemble and cook the lasagne.

Preheat the oven to 180°C/160°C fan/350°F/gas 4. Lightly butter the lasagne dish. Place a layer of Bolognese sauce on the base of the dish, followed by a layer of pasta, then some basil leaves on top and half the béchamel sauce. Repeat these four layers once more. End with a final third layer of pasta and top it with the rest of the Bolognese. Cover the dish with foil and bake in the preheated oven for 20 minutes. Slice the lasagne into portions and serve on warm plates. Be sure to have plenty of grated Grana Padano on hand for sprinkling over the lasagne.

*The time I had my first authentic lasagne Bolognese, I have to say, I was not particularly excited. Although I was placing the order in a well-respected trattoria called Tamburini, it was a hot day and my instinct was that it was too warm for eating lasagne. In the interest of research, however I ordered it, intending to take just a bite and leave. How wrong could I have been? It was light as a feather, utterly fragrant and so delicious I could have ordered more. When done properly, this lasagne can take up to 4 hours to make, but it is a labour of love that is very much worth it.*

# OPEN LASAGNE WITH VEGETABLES & OREGANO DRESSING

## LASAGNE APERTA

*Whenever I ask my students what is their favourite pasta dish, lasagne is a clear winner. Throughout this book there are three lasagne. This particular treatment is a firm favourite with my family; I hope you enjoy this as much as they do!*

**2 red (bell) peppers, deseeded and cut into thick strips**
**2 small aubergines/eggplants, halved lengthways and cut into thick slices**
**600 g/1 lb. 5 oz. butternut squash or firm pumpkin, peeled, deseeded and cut into wedges**
**200 g/7 oz. baby plum tomatoes**
**100 ml/scant 1/2 cup extra virgin olive oil**
**6 fresh bay leaves**
**1 1/2 teaspoons fennel seeds, lightly toasted and crushed**
**1 garlic clove, crushed**
**pinch of dried chilli flakes/hot red pepper flakes**
**small handful of fresh oregano, roughly chopped**
**2 teaspoons best-quality red wine vinegar**
**large handful of green olives, stoned/pitted**
**12 fresh lasagne sheets (see Note)**
**200 g/7 oz. mozzarella, drained and sliced**
**sea salt and freshly ground black pepper**
**handful of fresh basil leaves, to garnish**

**Serves 4**

Preheat the oven to 200°C/180°C fan/400°F/gas 6.

Divide the peppers, aubergines, squash and tomatoes between 2 large baking sheets. Drizzle each with 2 tablespoons of the olive oil to lightly coat, add the bay leaves and season well. Slide the trays into the centre of the preheated oven to roast the vegetables for about 35 minutes or until they have turned soft, burnished and sweet. Cover loosely with foil and set aside to keep warm.

Combine the remaining olive oil with the fennel seeds, garlic, chilli flakes, oregano, vinegar and olives to make a dressing. Season to taste.

To cook the lasagne sheets, bring a large saucepan of salted water to a rolling boil. Working two at a time, cook the pasta strips for 2 minutes. Using a slotted spoon, lift the par-cooked pasta strips out of the pan and lay them out on a clean dry tea/dish towel to drain.

On individual serving plates, layer the roasted vegetables, sliced mozzarella and olive oil dressing with the cooked lasagne sheets, artfully draping the pasta to make an attractive open lasagne. Finish each plate with a few fresh basil leaves to garnish.

**Note:** *To make your own lasagne sheets, follow the recipe for fresh egg pasta on page 73. Roll out the dough as thinly as you can manage (about 1 mm/1/16 inch thick) and then cut into 8 x 10-cm/3 1/4 x 4-inch lasagne sheets.*

# WHITE LASAGNE

## LASAGNE IN BIANCO

*This is a very celebratory, but also light and utterly divine dish. I am always proud to make and serve this lasagne to my family and friends, especially on a special occasion.*

**110 g/$^{1}/_{2}$ cup/1 stick unsalted butter, plus extra for greasing**
**1 onion, thinly sliced**
**200 g/1$^{1}/_{2}$ cups Italian 00 flour**
**2 teaspoons freshly grated nutmeg**
**750 ml/3 cups whole/full-fat milk**
**250 ml/1 cup chicken broth (see page 41)**
**2 large/US extra-large eggs, beaten**
**120 ml/$^{1}/_{2}$ cup dry Marsala**
**180 g/2 cups grated Parmigiano Reggiano**
**1 quantity fresh egg pasta dough (see page 73), made with 3 large/ US extra-large eggs and 300 g/ 2$^{1}/_{4}$ cups Italian 00 flour**
**sea salt and freshly ground black pepper**

*23 x 15-cm/9 x 6-inch baking dish*

**Serves 6**

Preheat the oven to 200°C/180°C fan/400°F/gas 6. Grease the baking dish with butter.

Melt the butter in a saucepan. Add the onion and cook over a low heat for about 5 minutes until softened but not coloured. Stir in the flour and cook over a medium heat for at least 4 minutes. Add the nutmeg, then slowly add the milk over a simmering heat until the sauce is thick enough to coat the back of a spoon. Pour in the broth and stir to mix well. Remove from the heat and leave to cool slightly.

Once cool, add the eggs, Marsala, half the grated Parmigiano Reggiano and season well with salt and pepper. Mix until the sauce is smooth.

Meanwhile, roll out the pasta dough as thinly as you can manage on a lighty floured surface (about 1 mm/$^{1}/_{16}$ inch thick) and then cut into sheets about 8–10 cm/3–4 inches wide and as long as your baking dish.

Working in batches, cook the lasagne sheets in a large saucepan of boiling salted water until al dente. Don't overcrowd the pan, cook just three strips at a time. Using tongs, lift the sheets out of the pan and lay them on clean tea/dish towels in a single layer while you continue cooking.

Cover the base of the baking dish with a shallow layer of the sauce and top with a layer of the cooked lasagne sheets. Spoon over another ladleful of the sauce, sprinkle with some of the remaining grated Parmigiano Reggiano and top with another layer of pasta. Repeat the first four layers again, finishing with a top layer of sauce and cheese. Bake in the preheated oven for 45 minutes until golden.

Slice the lasagne into portions, sprinkled with plenty of black pepper and serve on warm plates.

# PUMPKIN TORTELLI

## TORTELLI DI ZUCCA

*During my research for this book, I found an almost identical recipe to this one originating from Lombardy. Pumpkins grow just as well in Lombardy as they do in Parma due to the climate, so that may explain the duplication. I recommend the delica or crown prince squash varieties for the best results.*

**300 g/10½ oz. pumpkin, deseeded and cut into 2-cm/¾-inch cubes**
**1 quantity fresh egg pasta dough (see page 73)**
**100 g/1 cup grated Grana Padano, plus extra to serve**
**2 amaretti biscuits, crumbled**
**2 teaspoons freshly grated nutmeg**
**50 g/3½ tablespoons unsalted butter, melted**
**6–8 fresh sage leaves**
**sea salt and freshly ground black pepper**

*fluted ravioli cutter (optional)*

**Serves 3–4**

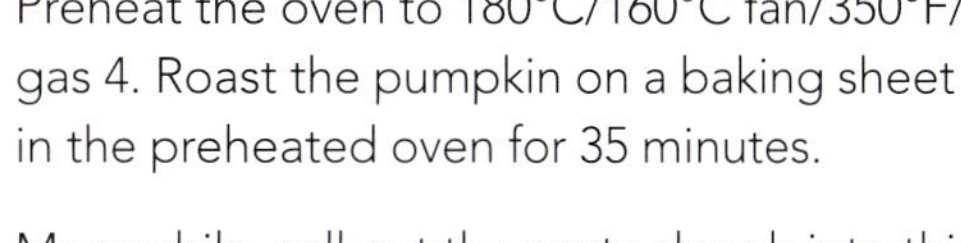

Preheat the oven to 180°C/160°C fan/350°F/gas 4. Roast the pumpkin on a baking sheet in the preheated oven for 35 minutes.

Meanwhile, roll out the pasta dough into thin sheets. If you are using a pasta machine, set it to number 8 (the one immediately before the last setting).

Combine the roasted pumpkin, grated Grano Padano, crumbled amaretti, nutmeg and some salt and pepper, then mix to a very smooth paste – it must be very smooth.

Cut the rolled-out pasta sheets into 6-cm/2½-inch squares. Using a teaspoon, put a mound of filling in the centre of each square. Brush a little water around the edges, then fold the square diagonally in half over the filling to make a triangular shape. Press to seal. Wrap the triangle around one of your index fingers, bringing the bottom two corners together and pinch the points to seal. Put the tortelli on a lightly floured clean tea/dish towel, sprinkle with more flour and leave to dry. Repeat the process with the remaining dough and filling.

Melt the butter in a saucepan, add the sage leaves and leave to infuse for 8–10 minutes.

To cook the pasta, bring a large saucepan of salted water to the boil. Drop the tortelli into the pan, bring the water back to the boil, reduce the heat and cook at a gentle simmer for 4 minutes or until cooked to your liking. Drain the tortelli and divide equally between warmed bowls. Spoon the sage-infused butter over the top and sprinkle with cheese to serve.

# QUADRETTI IN BROTH WITH CHICKEN LIVERS

## QUADRETTI IN BRODO CON I FEGATINI DI POLLO

*Quadretti is made from little pieces of fresh pasta dough, cut into small squares, but you can use store-bought pasta shapes if preferred. I use up any little pieces of leftover pasta dough for this dish and can think of no better way to celebrate pasta in the cooler months.*

**150 g/5½ oz. clean chicken livers**
**1 litre/4 cups chicken broth (see page 41)**
**1 garlic clove**
**4 fresh sage leaves**
**2 large rosemary sprigs**
**60 g/¼ cup/½ stick unsalted butter**
**200 g/7 oz. dried quadretti (I prefer the DeCecco brand) or fresh pasta, cut into 2-cm/¾-inch squares**
**large handful of finely chopped fresh flat-leaf parsley (optional)**
**50 g/⅔ cup grated Parmigiano Reggiano**
**sea salt and finely ground black pepper**

**Serves 4–6**

Place the chicken livers in a large saucepan with one-third of the broth, the garlic, sage and rosemary. Cook over a medium heat until the livers are browned, then remove them from the pan and chop into small pieces.

Remove and discard the garlic and herbs if you'd prefer a cleaner looking soup. Return the chicken livers to the pan. Add the butter and cook until bubbling. Season to taste.

In a large saucepan, bring the remaining broth to the boil, add the cooked livers and cook for 5 minutes. Add the quadretti and cook for a few more minutes until al dente. Add the parsley, if using, and stir well. Divide tequally between warmed bowls, then sprinkle over the grated Parmigiano Reggiano to serve and add more parsley if desired.

# TORTELLINI IN BROTH

## TORTELLINI IN BRODO

*If I had not included a recipe for* tortellini in brodo *in this book then it would not be a true representation of Emila-Romagna. It's a classic of the region, and for good reason. The authentic tortellini are actually incredibly small, about the size of a fingernail, but I have made mine slightly bigger for ease when shaping.*

**1 quantity fresh egg pasta dough (see page 73), made with 3 large/ US extra-large eggs and 300 g/ 2¼ cups Italian 00 flour**
**chopped fresh parsley, to serve (optional)**

BROTH
**300 g/10½ oz. beef shin**
**300 g/10½ oz. chicken thighs on the bone**
**1 onion**
**2 celery sticks/ribs**
**1 carrot**
**3 fresh bay leaves**
**3 whole cloves**
**1 ripe tomato, roughly chopped**

FILLING
**20 g/1½ tablespoons unsalted butter**
**100 g/3½ oz. finely minced/ground pork**
**40 g/½ cup Grana Padano, plus extra to serve**
**120 g/4½ oz. mortadella**
**120 g/4½ oz. prosciutto**
**½ teaspoon freshly ground nutmeg**
**1 large/US extra-large egg**
**salt and freshly ground black pepper**

**Serves 6–8**

To make the broth, place all the ingredients in a large saucepan or stock pot, cover with 2½ litres/quarts water, bring to the boil and then simmer for 3½–4 hours. Strain the broth through a fine-mesh sieve/strainer, then set aside until ready to use.

Wrap the pasta dough in cling film/plastic wrap and leave to rest for at least 20 minutes before rolling.

To make the filling, melt the butter in a pan and fry the pork until browned. Transfer to a bowl to cool before adding all the remaining ingredients. Season with salt and pepper. Transfer to a food processor and blitz to a paste.

Roll out the pasta dough into thin sheets, ideally 2-mm/⅛-inch thick. You can use either a rolling pin or a pasta machine – by hand is wonderful, but takes practice, whereas the pasta machine is foolproof. Cut the rolled-out pasta sheets into 5-cm/2-inch squares. Using a teaspoon, put a small mound of filling in the centre of each square. Brush a little water around the edges of each square, then fold the square diagonally in half over the filling to make a triangular shape. Press to seal. Wrap the triangle around one of your little fingers, bringing the bottom two corners together. Pinch the points together to seal. Finally, curl the upmost point backwards to give the classic tortellini shape.

Bring the broth for cooking the pasta to the boil in a large saucepan and season with salt and pepper. Add the tortellini to the pan and cook for 8 minutes. Divide the tortellini and broth between 6–8 warmed bowls and sprinkle with grated Grana Padano and chopped parsley to serve.

# STRANGOZZI WITH COURGETTE FLOWERS & CHICKEN

## STRANGOZZI CON FIORI DI ZUCCA E POLLO

*Strangozzi are a slightly smaller version of strozzapreti or 'priest stranglers', a special short pasta shape from Modena. Strangozzi is also known as 'shoelaces' because of its flat long shape. You can buy packets of them in Italian delicatessens, but if you can't find it then use gemelli, a similar kind of twisted pasta.*

**2 skinless chicken breasts (weighing about 350 g/12½ oz. in total)**
**50 g/3½ tablespoons unsalted butter**
**2 tablespoons olive oil**
**1 small onion, thinly sliced**
**200 g/7 oz. small courgettes/zucchini, cut into thin matchsticks**
**1 garlic clove, crushed**
**2 teaspoons finely chopped fresh marjoram**
**350 g/12½ oz. dried strangozzi**
**large handful of courgette/zucchini flowers, thoroughly washed and dried**
**sea salt and freshly ground black pepper**
**thinly shaved Parmigiano Reggiano, to serve**

**Serves 4**

Season the chicken with salt and pepper, then place under a medium grill/broiler and cook for 8 minutes, turning once, until lightly golden. Cut into evenly sized pieces and set aside until needed.

Heat the butter and half the olive oil in a saucepan, add the onion and cook gently, stirring frequently, for about 5 minutes until softened but not coloured.

Add the courgettes to the pan and sprinkle over the garlic and marjoram, then season with salt and pepper to taste. Add the chicken pieces to the pan and cook for 8 minutes until the courgettes have coloured.

Meanwhile, cook the strangozzi in a large saucepan of boiling salted water according to the instructions on the packet.

Set aside a few whole courgette flowers for the garnish, then roughly shred the rest and add them to the courgette mixture. Stir to mix, taste and adjust the seasoning as needed.

Drain the cooked pasta, tip it into a warmed serving bowl and add the remaining olive oil. Toss the pasta in the oil, add the courgette mixture and then toss again. Top with the Parmigiano Reggiano shavings and the reserved courgette flowers before serving.

# POTATO GNOCCHI

## GNOCCHI DI PATATE

*This dish is the reason I'm married – once eaten, never forgotten! The word gnocco, literally translated, means 'little lump', which is precisely what a gnocco is. There are so many poor imitations of gnocchi ready-prepared for us to buy, that I urge you to spend some time making them yourself. The results are infinitely superior, and it's certainly not difficult... in fact, it's fun! Old potatoes are best used here, rather than the waxy new ones, because the starch is fully developed, and therefore allows the gnocchi to cohere and stay together. The gnocchi are also lighter in texture. The classical way to enjoy potato gnocchi is with a homemade tomato sauce, or a walnut sauce, but they are even better with a Bolognese sauce.*

**900 g/2 lb. even-sized old potatoes (such as Maris Piper, King Edward or Desirée)**
**225–275 g/1¾–2 cups Italian 00 flour**
**2 small eggs**
**55 g/¼ cup/½ stick unsalted butter, softened and cut into cubes**
**sea salt**

TO SERVE
**½ quantity Bolognese sauce (see page 86), reheated**
**freshly grated Parmigiano Reggiano**

**Serves 6–8**

To make the gnocchi, cook the potatoes in their skins in a saucepan of boiling water for 20 minutes until tender (or longer, depending on size). Drain well and, when cool enough to handle, peel off the skins.

Sift the flour into a bowl and make a well in the centre. Crack the eggs into the well.

Push the potatoes through a fine-mesh sieve/strainer or a potato ricer onto the flour and eggs from a height to enable the potato to lighten with air as it falls. Season with plenty of salt and stir in the butter. Mix thoroughly and then knead to make a soft dough, adding more flour if necessary.

With floured hands, roll the dough into 2.5-cm/1-inch thick ropes, then cut each one into pieces about 2 cm/¾ inch long. Lightly press a finger into the centre of each piece to make an indentation, then draw your finger towards you to curl the sides.

Bring a large saucepan of salted water to the boil and drop in about 20 gnocchi. Lower the heat and cook gently for 2–3 minutes; once the gnocchi float to the surface of the water, count for 30 seconds. Remove the gnocchi from the pan with a slotted spoon, transfer to a bowl and keep warm. Repeat with the remaining gnocchi.

Divide the gnocchi equally between warmed bowls and serve with the Bolognese sauce and plenty of grated Parmigiano Reggiano to finish.

# PARMIGIANO REGGIANO RISOTTO

## RISOTTO ALLA PARMIGIANA DI MODENA

*I'm not sure there has ever been a more comforting dish to enjoy in the autumn when the weather turns chillier. The magnificent Parmigiano Reggiano is the star of the show here – such a powerful statement of a risotto.*

**80 g/1/3 cup/3/4 stick unsalted butter**
**6 shallots, finely chopped**
**400 g/14 oz. risotto rice (I use vialone nano)**
**1 litre/4 cups chicken broth** **(see page 41)**
**75 ml/1/3 cup white wine**
**300 g/3 3/4 cups grated Parmigiano Reggiano, plus extra to serve**
**sea salt and freshly ground black pepper**

**Serves 6**

In a sauté pan, melt 2 tablespoons of the butter and fry the shallots until golden. Add all the rice and stir well until every grain is coated in the butter. Gently cook until lightly coloured.

Reheat the broth so that it is the same temperature as the rice.

Add the wine to the pan, stir well and cook until the liquid has evaporated. Add the broth, one ladleful at a time, stirring continuously between additions as the broth is absorbed by the rice as it cooks. The should take 18–20 minutes.

Towards the end of the cooking, season well with the grated cheese, salt and pepper. Add the remaining butter, vigorously mixing it all into the rice. Remove from the heat and add one more ladleful of broth. Put a lid on the pan and let the risotto stand for a few minutes while you warm the bowls.

Ladle the risotto into the warmed bowls and serve with an abundance of grated Parmigiano Reggiano.

**Note:** *The finished risotto can also be garnished with finely chopped fresh flat-leaf parsley if desired.*

*Wheels of Parmigiano Reggiano that have been left to mature for an average of 24 months in a temperature-controlled environment.*

CHAPTER FOUR

# MEAT & FISH
# Carne e Pesce

*On the Adriatic Coast sits Cesenatico, a picturesque seaside town; running through the centre is the historic canal, lined with restaurants and bars serving fresh fish from the traditional fishing boats.*

# FROM THE LAND, SEA & RIVER

THE UNIQUE GEOGRAPHY of Emilia-Romagna, situated between the Po Valley and the Apennines, is a major factor in its food productivity. The fertile plains are where soft wheat for the local pasta is grown, and where cattle, sheep, pigs and poultry are farmed. These plains are hot and humid in the summer, cold in the winter. The foothills of the mountains are where you will find game animals and birds, fruit orchards, mushrooms and grapes for wines. Here the climate is less intensely hot, because of the elevation, but there is a lot of snow in the winter. On the Adriatic coast, the climate is gentle, more Mediterranean in feel, and here of course, is where the region's seafood – and salt – comes from. With such geographical and weather diversity, it's no wonder that Emilia-Romagnan ingredients are so delicious.

As you might guess, in a region famed for its porcine delicacies, the pig reigns supreme. Pork is found mainly in the preserved *salumi*, but two main-course fresh uses stand out: *zampone* and *cotechino*. *Zampone*, a Modena speciality, consists of a pig's trotter, which is cooked and boned, then filled with a mixture of spiced minced pork. *Cotechino* is a large and delicious pork sausage that also originated in the Modena area. It was said to have been 'invented' during the siege of the city-state of Mirandola in 1511, when the besieged had to eke out every last bit of the pigs' meat, making them into sausages. However, as the siege only lasted 17 days, I think this a little unlikely. Both *zampone* and *cotechino* are usually served with lentils or *sauerkraut* (a northern influence), polenta or mashed potatoes, and are popular at Christmas. *Cotechino in galera* (see page 118) is even more special for a New Year party: the sausage is wrapped in a thin slice of beef and braised in red wine.

Rich braises are a theme of Emilia-Romagnan cooking. *Bollito misto* is very popular here – a mixture of meats, literally, cooked together and served with savoury *mostarda* and *salsa verde*. Pork loin is braised in milk, *maiale al latte*, as is a large piece of beef, in *stracotto* (see page 125): this dish used to be made with horsemeat in Piacenza, but my beef version from Parma will be easier to source. Veal is cooked all over Italy, but I have found and reproduced some delicious provincial recipes here, one of which uses the wonderful local balsamic vinegar in its sauce (see page 126). Sheep meat is not all that common in Italy, but sheep are bred in Emilia-Romagna and sold as lamb and mutton, and both can be found grilled, roasted and braised. Grilled meats – mutton, sausages, ham and pork (particularly the meat of a local pig, the *mora romagnola*) – are popular in and around Ravenna.

Poultry dishes abound too, and of course a primary use of chicken is in making the wonderful broths (see page 41) in which many of the region's pastas are cooked. Chicken and chicken livers are used in pasta sauces too. Chicken could be cooked in the same way as veal in a couple of the recipes here, and rabbit could be cooked *alla cacciatore* (see page 112), with red wine, herbs, olives and capers – to be served, as in Modena, with *crescentini*. All of these main-course dishes with sauces should, by local tradition, be accompanied by bread of some sort, primarily to *fare la scarpetta* ('mop up the sauce').

Fish and seafood naturally dominate the menus of the seaside restaurants along the Adriatic coast. Fishing has been a way of life for hundreds of years, with villages and communities dedicated to searching for and selling individual types. Here you can buy, cook and eat mullet, sand smelts, sardines, anchovies, shrimps and flat fish like plaice and sole. Cesenatico is renowned for its mussels and other shellfish, while in Cervia you might get some fresh tuna straight off the boats (plus salt produced in local salt pans). In the small village of Bellaria-Igea Marina, the fishermen bring home clams, cuttlefish and sea snails, and Cattolica is known for its clams, mackerel, sardines and anchovies. Rimini, with the largest fish market in the region, sells everything piscine that you might want, but when there you must try an oily fish unique to the Adriatic, the *saraghina*, neither sardine nor anchovy, which is breadcrumbed and grilled. (Federico Fellini, the film director, who was born in Rimini, named one of the characters in his famous film *8½* after the fish.) A favoured method of cooking all of these fish is grilled, preferably over charcoal, and many fish, particularly the *saraghina*, are served wrapped in the local flatbread *piadini*.

Eating fish is popular here in the summer months particularly, as fish is lighter on the digestion, something all Italians are passionate about. Fish are used in soups

here, very like the *brodetti* offered along all Italian coastlines, and you might find an omelette with whitebait, a fish sauce on pasta, or a risotto with crab, snails or eel. Eel is one of the major ingredients of the area: it is fished along the entire Adriatic coast, but mostly in and around Comacchio, a historic town on the watery Po delta. Built on more than thirteen small islands, all connected by bridges, it is known as 'Little Venice'. If you visit, you will marvel at the historic *padelloni* or *bilancioni*; little huts with huge nets to one side, to be lowered into the water to catch fish. The main industry is eel fishing, and the fish are marinated, grilled, stewed, cooked in soup, preserved and canned.

I haven't given an eel recipe here, as it is not easy to find, but it is hugely popular in Italy. The Neapolitans love to serve *capitone* – a female eel – on Christmas Eve, and apparently in America, Italian communities hold *La Festa dei Sette Pesci* ('Feast of the Seven Fishes), which includes eel, on the same evening, based on the Catholic tradition of abstaining from meat on the night before a notable feast day.

# HUNTER-STYLE CHICKEN

## POLLO ALLA CACCIATORA

*I firmly believe every region in Italy has their very own version of this delightful chicken casserole. As the weather turns, it is so comforting and welcoming. My Emilia-Romagna version is quite different from my nonna's. I hope you like this one.*

- **750 g/1 lb. 10 oz. bone-in chicken thighs, skin removed**
- **2 tablespoons finely chopped fresh rosemary**
- **3 garlic cloves, finely chopped**
- **75 g/2¾ oz. pancetta**
- **2 tablespoons olive oil**
- **200 ml/generous ¾ cup dry red wine**
- **400-g/14-oz. can plum tomatoes**
- **20 green olives, stoned/pitted**
- **1 tablespoon capers**
- **handful of fresh flat-leaf parsley, finely chopped**
- **sea salt and freshly ground black pepper**
- **country-style bread, to serve**

**Serves 4–6**

Season the chicken all over with plenty of salt and pepper and place in a bowl with the rosemary and garlic. Toss everything together so the chicken is well coated with the herbs and seasonings. Leave covered in the fridge for at least 3 hours for the flavours to infuse the meat.

Chop the pancetta into cubes, then gently fry in a shallow pan over a low heat to release some of its fat. When the pancetta is nicely browned, add the oil and then the chicken and cook, turning occasionally to keep it moving, until browned on all sides.

Add the wine and continue cooking until the liquid evaporates. Add the tomatoes, olives and capers and cook for about 45 minutes over a low heat. Keep checking during the cooking and top up with a little water if the casserole look dry. When ready, the chicken meat should be falling away from the bones.

Taste and adjust the seasoning with more salt and pepper to taste. Scatter over the chopped parsley to finish. Serve with some good bread on the side.

# PAN-FRIED DUCK WITH BALSAMIC VINEGAR

## ANATRA CON ACETO BALSAMICO

*Although I have previously included a recipe for duck in both my books on Veneto and Sicily, I decided to include another here. When visiting Bologna I sampled a very scrumptious pan-fried duck dish, typical of that region. Providing the ingredients are all of a very high quality, including the balsamic vinegar, this is really wonderful and yet easy to make.*

**3 duck breasts, each weighing about 400 g/14 oz.**
**2 hearts of radicchio, quartered lengthways**
**4 tablespoons best-quality balsamic vinegar, or more to taste**
**sea salt and freshly ground black pepper**
**country-style bread, to serve**

**Serves 6**

Cut the duck breasts in half widthways. Score the skin with the tip of a small, sharp knife, then rub with salt and pepper.

Heat a heavy-based frying pan/skillet over a medium heat. Place the duck breasts in the pan, skin side down, and cook for about 9 minutes, depending on the thickness of the meat, until the skin is golden and the meat remains pink in the middle. Pour away most of the rendered duck fat from the pan.

Meanwhile, preheat the grill/broiler to a high heat. Place the quartered radicchio under the hot grill for 7 minutes, turning occasionally until lightly charred.

Spoon 1 tablespoon of the balsamic vinegar over the duck breasts, then turn and cook for a further 2 minutes on the other side. Transfer the duck breasts to a board, cover with foil and set aside to rest.

Meanwhile, add the remaining balsamic vinegar and along with 3 tablespoons water to the pan and stir well to deglaze, scraping the sediment off the bottom of the pan. Taste and adjust the seasoning with more salt or pepper and balsamic vinegar if needed.

Cut the duck crossways into 1-cm/½-inch slices and arrange on warmed serving plates with the chargrilled radicchio, then drizzle with the balsamic pan juices. Serve with some good bread to mop up the delicious juices.

# BRAISED LAMB CUTLETS WITH ONIONS, HERBS & OLIVES

## COSTOLETTE DI AGNELLO CON CIPOLLE E OLIVE

*I picked up this dish during my time in Ravenna. It is a magnificent way to cook lamb low and slow, which works especially well if it is not spring lamb. The onions are cooked to a melting sweetness, while the black olives enrich the dish and give it a smoky taste. The cutlets can be finished off in a medium–hot oven instead of cooking on the stovetop. They are also very good reheated.*

**8–12 lamb cutlets or chops, depending on size**
**100 ml/scant 1/2 cup olive oil**
**1 kg/2 1/4 lb. onions, thinly sliced**
**2 tablespoons chopped fresh rosemary, plus extra sprigs to serve**
**2 tablespoons chopped fresh oregano**
**4 anchovy fillets in oil, drained, rinsed and chopped**
**15 stoned/pitted black olives**
**sea salt and freshly ground black pepper**

**Serves 4**

Season the lamb cutlets on both sides with salt and pepper.

Heat half the oil in a large frying pan/skillet until very hot, then add the cutlets and quickly brown on both sides. Remove to a plate and leave to cool.

Heat the remaining oil in the same pan and add the onions. Cook over a gentle heat for 15 minutes, stirring occasionally, until the onions begin to soften, but do not let them brown. Stir in the chopped herbs, anchovies and olives, then season with salt and pepper to taste.

Return the cutlets to the pan, arranging them on top of the bed of onions, and cover with a lid. Cook over a very low heat for 20 minutes, checking regularly to make sure that the onions do not catch and burn. Scatter over a few rosemary sprigs before serving at the table direct from the pan.

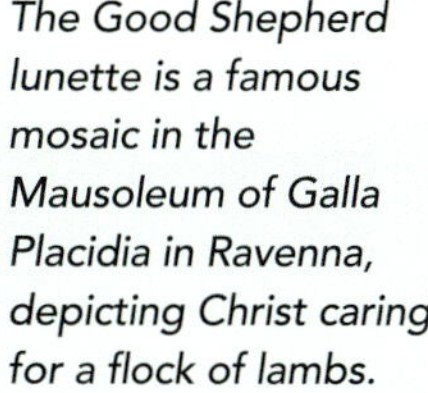

*The Good Shepherd lunette is a famous mosaic in the Mausoleum of Galla Placidia in Ravenna, depicting Christ caring for a flock of lambs.*

# COTECHINO IN JAIL

## COTECHINO IN GALERA

*Cotechino is a unique pork sausage specifically from the Modena region, however it can be bought from delicatessans and online. It is simply prepared, usually boiled and served with lentils, but here it is cooked* in galera *(in jail) because the sausagemeat is imprisoned in the rolled beef.*

- 1 kg/2¼ lb. cotechino (hearty pork sausage)
- 1 thick slice of raw beef (weighing about 500 g/1 lb. 2oz.), big enough to wrap around the cotechino (normally sirloin)
- 50 g/3½ tablespoons unsalted butter
- 2 onions, thinly sliced
- 100 ml/scant ½ cup dry red wine
- 200 ml/scant 1 cup beef broth (see page 41)
- cooked green or Puy lentils, to serve (optional)

### Serves 6

*The medieval fortress, La Rocca di Vignola, is situated in the oldest part of the town.*

Place the cotechino in a large saucepan and pour in enough water to cover. Bring to the boil and cook the cotechino for 30 minutes. Leave to cool, then remove the skin, taking care not to break up the sausagemeat.

Put the slice of beef on a chopping board and place the cotechino on top. Wrap the beef around the sausage to encase it and tie in place with cooking string or twine.

Melt the butter in a pan big enough to hold the cotechino. Add the onions and gently fry them for 5–10 minutes until golden. Add the wine and wrapped cotechino to the pan, then cook, covered, for 1 hour, adding the beef broth as needed to prevent the sausage drying up. There should be a thin layer of cooking juices and onions in the bottom of the pan.

When ready to serve, cut the cotechino into thick slices and warm through the lentils. Serve the cotechino while hot on a bed of lentils with the onions and sauce spooned over the top.

# STUFFED VEAL ROLLS

## INVOLTINI DI VITELLO

*I really love veal. It is the favourite meat of Northern Italy. Not only is it of outstanding value, it is light on ones digestion and absorbs flavours well. This is the perfect summer celebratory dish.*

**12 slices of veal (weighing 1 kg/2¼ lb. in total), 6 mm/¼ inch thick**
**80 g/⅓ cup/¾ stick unsalted butter**
**3 tablespoons olive oil**
**1 onion, finely chopped**
**12 slices of prosciutto**
**180 g/2 cups grated Grana Padano**
**30 g/4 tablespoons Italian 00 flour, seasoned with salt and pepper**
**100 ml/scant ½ cup dry white wine**
**sea salt and freshly ground black pepper**

TO GARNISH

**4 tomatoes, deseeded and roughly chopped**
**handful of fresh basil leaves**

**Serves 6**

Preheat the oven to 160°C/140°C fan/325°F/gas 3.

Heat a shallow ovenproof pan big enough to hold the *involtini* (or use two if necessary). Add half the butter and all the oil and warm over a gentle heat. Add the onion and cook for about 5 minutes until lightly coloured, but not brown.

Meanwhile, top each piece of veal with a slice of prosciutto, a little cheese and a dot of butter. Roll the veal to encase the filling. Coat the *involtini* in the flour.

Add the *involtini* to the pan with the onion and colour them on all sides. Add the wine and 200 ml/scant 1 cup water, then allow the liquid to reduce by half. Transfer the pan to the preheated oven and continue cooking the *involtini* for 20 minutes. The alcohol in the wine will evaporate to leave some wonderful pan juices.

When ready to serve, divide the *involtini* between warmed plates, spoon over the pan juices and garnish with the tomatoes. Finally, scatter over a few basil leaves.

# VEAL ESCALOPES BOLOGNESE-STYLE

## SCALOPPINE DI VITELLO ALLA BOLOGNESE

*As a fan of veal, I am thrilled that it is now more readily available and ethically farmed. This Bolognese dish is very similar to the Roman classic,* saltimbocca. *Both are utterly divine.*

**2 tablespoons Italian 00 flour, seasoned with salt and pepper**
**50 g/3½ tablespoons unsalted butter**
**4 veal escalopes**
**2 tablespoons dry white wine**
**4 slices of prosciutto**
**75 g/¾ cup grated Grana Padano**
**sea salt and freshly ground black pepper**

**Serves 4**

Preheat the oven to 180°C/160°C fan/350°F/gas 4.

Coat the veal escalopes in the seasoned flour.

Melt the butter in a large ovenproof frying pan/skillet that will hold the veal escalopes without overcrowding the pan. Add the veal and cook until golden on both sides. This depends on the thickness of the meat.

Add the wine to the pan, then allow the liquid to reduce by half.

Lay a slice of prosciutto on each escalope and sprinkle over all the cheese. Transfer the pan to the preheated oven and continue cooking the veal for 12 minutes. Serve immediately while hot.

*Pictured on page 6.*

# ROAST CHICKEN WITH BROAD BEANS & LEMON

## POLLO ARROSTO CON FAVE E LIMONE

*I adore broad/fava beans and grow them each year with varying degrees of success. They pair well with chicken (my husband's favourite) to make an easy, relaxed summer lunch. Earthy, tasty and colourful, this dish is simply divine when served with lemon and parsley mash. I ate something very similar when lunching with friends in Bologna.*

**375 g/3¼ cups fresh shelled broad/fava beans**
**2 tablespoons olive oil**
**1.5 kg/3¼ lb. chicken pieces (thighs or legs), bone in, skin on**
**3 onions, roughly chopped**
**handful of fresh thyme sprigs**
**zest and juice of 2 unwaxed lemons**
**3 garlic cloves, thinly sliced**
**350 ml/1⅓ cups chicken stock (see page 41)**
**handful of fresh mint leaves**
**2 tablespoons capers, drained and rinsed**
**sea salt and freshly ground black pepper**

**Serves 4**

Preheat the oven to 200°C/180°C fan/400°F/gas 6.

Bring a large pan of water to the boil. Add the broad beans and boil for 2 minutes. Drain and refresh under cold running water. Peel the skins from the beans and discard.

Heat the oil in a large ovenproof casserole dish/Dutch oven over a high heat. Working in batches, cook the chicken pieces for 4 minutes on each side until browned. Remove from the dish and set aside.

Add the onions, thyme and lemon zest to the casserole dish and cook for 2 minutes. Return the chicken and any juices to the dish with the garlic and stock. Bring to the boil, then season salt and pepper. Transfer to the preheated oven and cook uncovered for 40 minutes.

Stir in the broad beans along with 2 tablespoons lemon juice. Scatter over the mint and capers, then season with salt and pepper to taste. Serve immediately.

# PARMA'S POT ROAST

## STRACOTTO DI MANZO DI PARMA

*There are many regional variations on the pot roast, but this is the one that I happen to love the most. The inclusion of tomatoes is what characterizes the Parmigiano version. I have served this dish at many dinner parties; it is excellent with soft polenta or gnocchi.*

**30 g/2 tablespoons unsalted butter**
**3 tablespoons olive oil**
**1.5 kg/3¼ lb. beef shoulder or rump**
**50 g/scant ½ cup Italian 00 flour, seasoned with salt and pepper**
**1 onion, diced**
**1 celery stick/rib, diced**
**1 carrot, peeled and diced**
**4 garlic cloves, finely chopped**
**handful of fresh flat-leaf parsley**
**3 fresh bay leaves**
**6 fresh sage leaves**
**1 bottle good red wine (preferably Colli di Parma Rosso)**
**300 g/10½ oz. canned chopped tomatoes**
**1 litre/4 cups beef broth (see page 41)**
**sea salt and freshly ground black pepper**

TO SERVE
**handful of fresh flat-leaf parsley**
**Parmigiano Reggiano, grated**
**gnocchi or polenta**

**Serves 4–6**

Preheat the oven to 150°C/130°C fan/300°F/gas 3.

Melt the butter with the oil in a deep roasting pan or casserole dish/Dutch oven over a medium heat. Dredge the beef in the seasoned flour and then add it to the pan with the onion, celery, carrot and garlic. Cook for about 10 minutes until the vegetables have softened and the beef has browned all over.

Add the parsley, bay leaves, sage leaves, red wine, chopped tomatoes and broth to the pan, cover with foil or the lid and transfer to the preheated oven to cook for 3½–4 hours until the beef is tender and yielding.

Mash the roasted vegetables in the pan, then sprinkle over more parsley and Parmigiano. Serve slices of the beef and the mashed vegetables with your choice of gnocchi or polenta.

*A detail of an early Christian mosaic pavement from an old building in the Chiesa di San Giovanni Evangelista, Ravenna.*

# BALSAMIC VEAL

## VITELLO CON ACETO BALSAMICO

*This classic veal dish from Modena could not be simpler to make. If you cannot find veal, then chicken may be used instead and is equally tasty. Serve this casserole with either soft polenta or mashed potatoes on the side.*

**50 g/3½ tablespoons unsalted butter**
**2 red onions, finely chopped**
**1 carrot, finely chopped**
**2 celery stalks/ribs, finely chopped**
**4 plum tomatoes, skinned and chopped**
**400 g/14 oz. veal, cut into cubes**
**100 g/3½ oz. pancetta**
**15 g/½ oz. dried porcini, soaked in water for 20 minutes and chopped into small pieces**
**pinch of ground cinnamon**
**3 fresh bay leaves**
**3 tablespoons best-quality balsamic vinegar**
**sea salt and freshly ground black pepper**
**chopped fresh flat-leaf parsley, to garnish (optional)**

**Serves 4–6**

Heat the butter in a casserole dish/Dutch oven or sauté pan with a lid. Add the onions, carrot and celery, then cook until browned. Add the tomatoes, then the veal and pancetta and cook over a low heat for about 5–7 minutes. Add the soaked porcini, cinnamon and bay leaves and season well. Finally, stir in the vinegar and cook over a low heat for 1 hour with the lid on the pan.

After an hour, check the veal to make sure it is tender, then taste and adjust the seasoning if needed. When ready to serve, garnish with a generous handful of parsley, if desired.

# PLAICE & CAVOLO NERO ROLLS

## ROTOLO DI PLATESSA AL CAVOLO

*I recently had the opportunity to ask a chef who lives in Bologna what is his favourite restaurant. Without hesitation he replied Ristorante Diana. By luck, I stumbled across that very restaurant on the way from my hotel to the Pied Saint Neptuno. I just had to go inside. It really was outstanding. I hope you enjoy my attempt to replicate what I ate in that amazing restaurant.*

**15 g/1 tablespoon butter**
**1 shallot, finely chopped**
**1 garlic clove, thinly sliced**
**1 tablespoon chopped fresh flat-leaf parsley**
**1 tablespoon chopped fresh lemon thyme**
**50 g/1 cup fresh breadcrumbs**
**4 sun-dried tomatoes, roughly chopped**
**juice of 1 unwaxed lemon**
**8 large cabbage leaves (preferably cavalo nero)**
**8 plaice fillets**
**olive oil, to drizzle**
**sea salt and freshly ground black pepper**
**lemon wedges, to garnish**

**Serves 4**

Preheat the oven to 180°C/160°C fan/ 350°F/gas 4.

First, make the filling. Place the butter in a frying pan/skillet and let it melt over a low heat. Add the shallot and gently fry until golden. Add the garlic, chopped herbs, breadcrumbs, sun-dried tomatoes and lemon juice, then season with salt and pepper to taste. Set aside to cool.

Cook the cabbage leaves in a large saucepan of boiling water for 2 minutes, then plunge into iced water. Pat dry with paper towels.

Place a cabbage leaf on a chopping board, lightly season with salt and pepper, then sit a plaice fillet on top. Next, place a small ball of the cold stuffing mixture at one end of the place. Starting at one end, roll up the cabbage leaf and plaice fillet together, with the cabbage on the outside. Repeat with the remaining cabbage leaves and plaice fillets to make 12 rolls.

Arrange the cabbage and plaice rolls in an ovenproof baking dish in a single layer, drizzle with oil cover with foil. Bake the rolls in the preheated oven for 12 minutes. Serve with lemon wedges for squeezing over.

# MULLET STEW

## CEFALI IN UMIDO

*A wonderful selection of fish is available all along the Adriatic coast, a significant part of which lies within the Emilia-Romagna region. One of these fish is red mullet that can be very simply cooked using this uncomplicated method.*

**2 whole red mullet, each weighing about 250 g/9 oz.**
**50 g/6 tablespoons Italian 00 flour**
**3 tablespoons olive oil**
**4 ripe tomatoes, peeled and diced**
**2 salted anchovy fillets, minced**
**generous sprig of fresh rosemary**
**sea salt and freshly ground black pepper**
**crusty bread, to serve**

**Serves 2**

Gut and clean the mullet, then pat dry with paper towels. Sprinkle the fish with flour on both sides.

Heat a large frying pan/skillet over a high heat and add the oil. Once hot, place the mullet in the pan, turn down the heat to medium and gently cook on both sides to not break the fish.

When the mullet is golden, add the tomatoes, anchovies, rosemary and some black pepper. Add a couple of spoonfuls of water to prevent the fish drying out. Cover the pan with a lid and cook over a medium heat for 20 minutes. When the eyes are white, the fish is ready.

Carefully lift the mullet onto individual plates, then spoon over lots of the tomato sauce. Serve with good bread for mopping up the sauce.

# GRILLED SARDINES WITH FRESH TOMATO SALAD

## SARDE CON CRUDAIOLA DI POMODORI

*This the perfect treatment for oily fish like sardines, which I first enjoyed in the fishing town of Cattolica on the coast of Emilia-Romagna. I highly recommend using fresh sardines for this dish. And make more than you need – it is so good, you will become addicted!*

**1 kg/2¼ lb. firm ripe tomatoes**
**1 tablespoon red wine vinegar**
**handful of fresh flat-leaf parsley, roughly chopped**
**bunch of fresh basil leaves, roughly torn**
**1 tablespoon mild extra virgin olive oil**
**8 fat sardines, gutted and scales removed**
**zest and juice of 1 unwaxed lemon**
**sea salt freshly ground black pepper**
**lemon wedges, to serve**

**Serves 4**

First, make the sauce. Plunge the tomatoes into a bowl of boiling water and leave for 30 seconds. Remove with a slotted spoon. The skins should pop off obediently if the tomatoes are ripe. Remove the seeds and cut into slices.

Put the tomato slices in a bowl and salt well. Add the vinegar and black pepper, mix well, then add the parsley and basil and dress with olive oil. Set aside.

Arrange the sardines in an ovenproof baking dish in a single layer. Add the lemon zest and juice.

Preheat the grill/broiler to high. Grill the sardines until the eyes of the fish turn white and the skin starts to blister. Depending on the size of the sardines, this is usually quite quick so keep an eye on them while they cook.

Serve the grilled sardines with the tomato salad and some lemon wedges for squeezing over.

# GRIDDLED TUNA STEAKS WITH FENNEL

## TONNO MARINATO CON FINOCCHIO

*A lasting food memory is of enjoying this dish during a business trip to Ravenna with my father. Business was conducted not in an office or in a restaurant, but rather in a fish market and then in the car, followed by a kitchen where this dish was prepared for us. It was an unforgettable lunch of the most memorable food and convivial hospitality.*

**4 x 125-g/4½-oz. tuna steaks**
**2 fennel bulbs, thinly sliced lengthways**
**2 red onions, thinly sliced**
**2–3 tablespoons olive oil**
**crusty bread, to serve**

MARINADE
**125 ml/½ cup extra virgin olive oil**
**4 fresh red chillies/chiles, deseeded and finely chopped**
**4 garlic cloves, crushed**
**grated zest and freshly squeezed juice of 3 unwaxed lemons**
**25 g/1 oz. fresh flat-leaf parsley, finely chopped**
**sea salt and freshly ground black pepper**

**Serves 4**

For the marinade, mix all the ingredients together in a bowl and season to taste.

For the tuna, place the steaks in a shallow dish and cover with 2–3 spoonfuls of the marinade for about 5 minutes. Reserve the remaining marinade.

Place a griddle/grill pan or heavy-based frying pan/skillet over a medium heat. Toss the fennel and onions with the oil, then cook for 5 minutes until softened. Transfer to a plate and drizzle with the reserved marinade.

Remove the tuna steaks from the marinade and sear in the griddle pan or frying pan over a high heat for about 4–5 minutes on each side until opaque on the outside but still slightly pink in the middle, depending on the thickness of the steaks.

Serve the tuna steaks on top of the vegetables along with some crusty bread to soak up the juices.

# BRAISED TROUT IN RED WINE VINEGAR

## TROTA ALL'ACETO ROSSO

*Italy has a reputation for its fish dishes. While the coastal regions have a range of trawled fish and seafood, even landlocked regions enjoy fish caught in lakes and rivers. Parma is dependent on its rivers – the Po and Taro – that run through the region as well as its small lakes. Anglers are a familiar sight at the water's edge and trout is the most commonly available catch on offer.*

*My husband frequently brings home a fresh trout from the River Test, in Hampshire in the UK, so I often prepare trout in this way; it really is the best way to cook it.*

**2 x 500-g/1 lb. 2-oz. whole trout, gutted and scaled**
**60 g/½ cup Italian 00 flour, seasoned with sea salt and freshly ground black pepper**
**80 ml/⅓ cup olive oil**
**60 ml/¼ cup red wine vinegar**
**1 small shallot, finely chopped**
**handful of fresh flat-leaf parsley, roughly chopped**

**Serves 4**

Dredge the trout with the seasoned flour.

Preheat the oven to 160°C/140°C fan/320°F/gas 3.

Heat the oil in a shallow ovenproof pan that can hold both the trout. Add the fish to the pan and brown on both sides over a medium heat. Pour the vinegar into the pan over the trout and let it sizzle for at least 40 seconds.

Transfer the pan to the preheated oven and bake the trout for 20 minutes. When the eyes are white, the fish is ready.

Transfer the trout to a serving plate, then pour over the pan juices, garnish with the shallot and parsley before serving.

*The salt storehouses in Cervia are two historic warehouses located along the canal harbour. One is now home to the MUSA Salt Museum, which documents the traditional method of salt production in the Ravenna region.*

CHAPTER FIVE

# VEGETABLES
## Verdura

*The Po Valley is affectionately known as 'the breadbasket' of Italy as it is famous for the cultivation of wheat and maize, as well as being Europe's largest producer of risotto rice.*

# AN ABUNDANCE OF FRESHNESS

ITALIANS LOVE VEGETABLES so much that there used to be – and occasionally still is, in more expensive restaurants or at special feasts – an actual vegetable course as part of a formal meal. This comes traditionally after the *antipasti*, pasta and main course, and was considered to be a digestif. Many of the recipes here could be served so, but also have other uses: they can be an *antipasto*, or an accompaniment to a plate of meat or fish. Because I don't eat much meat, quite often I have a delicious vegetable dish by itself as my main (and only) course for lunch or dinner.

Much of Emilia-Romagna lies in the fertile valley of the great Po River, so the produce is similar to that of the Veneto, its north-eastern neighbour. Vegetables that grow well in the region include shallots, onions, garlic, potatoes, artichokes, tomatoes, asparagus, sweet bell peppers and squash. The Romagna shallot – *scalogno di Romagna* – has a stronger and more fragrant flavour than onion, and it is sweeter too. Grown around Bologna and Ravenna, it can be used in traditional pasta and meat sauces, or baked whole. The Bologna potato, of the Primura variety, has a yellow skin and dense yellow flesh – it is good for salads, as well as for baking and roasting. Voghiera garlic, grown near Ferrara, is sweet and flavourful, but not too strong. (It can be found as black garlic too, created by a fermentation process, which renders the flesh more balsamic vinegar/soy sauce-like in flavour.) The three vegetables above, the shallot, potato and garlic, have DOP (see page 8).

Globe artichokes are also a speciality of the region: the *violetta di Romagna* is famous for its lilac leaves and supreme taste; the Moretto artichoke from the town of Brisighella has a slightly bitter flavour. My recipe on page 24 combines these famous artichokes, plucked while small, with mint and anchovies. Green asparagus and pumpkin are found too, the latter used especially in the fillings for pasta such as *tortelli*, but also in *gnocchi*, soups, risottos, baked and fried, and even cakes. Local onions and tomatoes are cooked down together for an amazingly tasty sauce, *friggione* (see page 151), which can be served as an *antipasto*, either as a dip with fresh or fried bread, or as an accompaniment for grilled meats or cheese. (It has been used as a pasta sauce too.) The famous *melanzane alla Parmigiana* (see page 155) is quintessentially from Parma, using the local cheese and aubergines in the most delicious dish. And don't let us forget the vegetables that are picked to be pickled or otherwise preserved for use throughout the winter. The most famous version in Emilia-Romagna is known as *giardiniera* (see page 31), which is served with *salumi* and other products as *antipasti*.

The Italians in general love stuffing foods, and it is particularly popular in Emilia-Romagna. Not only do cooks fill billowy pasta cases with savoury stuffings, they also use and fill a variety of vegetables, such as onions, courgettes/zucchini – a speciality of Bologna, where the local *zucchini* are small and pot-bellied – aubergines/eggplant and sweet bell peppers. On Twelfth Night, when it is traditional to avoid meat, many Emilian families eat stuffed cabbage, *verzolini della vigilia* (see page 159). Pastry is also 'stuffed': *erbazzone* is a famous Emilian savoury pie of greens, bacon and cheese in a lard pastry. Bread too is stuffed in the region, particularly the famous *piadina* (see page 37), the flatbread that can actually be folded to a half-moon shape over a filling before baking (when it is known as *cassone* or *crescione*), or used, cooked, to wrap around a variety of ingredients such as cured meats, vegetables or cheeses (or, for a sweet version, jam or Nutella).

All the vegetables mentioned above are grown in the fertile soil of the Po Valley, but the southern half of the region, where the Apennines mark the boundary between Emilia-Romagna and Tuscany, is important too. Here in the foothills and higher you will find the wild mushrooms about which Italians are so passionate, and orchards of fruits and sweet chestnut trees. Chestnuts have figured in Emilian cooking for centuries, so much so that the tree is often referred to as the *albero del pane* or 'bread tree'. The nuts are eaten roasted, boiled and ground to make flour for cakes, pancakes, polenta, pasta and *gnocchi*. Black and white truffles are also occasionally found up here, and are used in dishes such as the ancient *pasticcio alla ferrarese* (a pie from Ferrara filled with béchamel sauce, a white meat ragú, macaroni and truffle). Truffles are a rare treat for me....

Fruits also feature in Emilia-Romagnan agriculture and cooking, particularly peaches, plums, apricots, quinces, apples and pears (often used in the local

*mostarda*). But the primary fruit in this region, which plays a huge role all over Italy, is the grape. Vineyards proliferate in Emilia-Romagna, and many good wines are produced, but the primary and most famous grape product here is the superb balsamic vinegar of Modena.

Traditional and genuine balsamic vinegar is produced only in Emilia-Romagna, in Modena and Reggio Emilia. Three types are produced: the DOP 'traditional' vinegars of both Modena and Reggio Emilia, and the IGP vinegar of Modena (see page 8). The juice of newly picked and squeezed white grapes, usually white Trebbiano or Lambrusco, is boiled down to a sugary must. This thick syrup – *mosto cotto* – is then put in barrels to age for a minimum of 12 years, and up to at least 25 years for the DOP vinegars. (The IGP vinegar can be aged for up to 6 years, when it is designated 'aged'.) The flavour intensifies over the years, becoming sweet, viscous and very concentrated. The barrels used (as in whisky making) are of different woods, all of which can contribute to the flavour of the barrel contents. You can probably appreciate now, why 'traditional' balsamic vinegar is so expensive to buy. Use it carefully and minimally, to add enormous flavour to many foods: you will find a few instances in this book, but also think of using just a drop in a salad dressing or on a piece of aged Parmigiano Reggiano to truly appreciative its wonderful flavour.

# STUFFED COURGETTES

## ZUCCHINI FARCITI

*I cannot think of a better way to prepare courgettes/zucchini, particularly in summer when there can be glut – they are bursting with flavour and look so pretty on the plate.*

**6 courgettes/zucchini**
**350 g/12½ oz. ricotta**
**2 large/US extra-large eggs, beaten**
**2 garlic cloves, grated**
**3 tablespoons chopped fresh basil**
**grated zest of ½ unwaxed lemon**
**6 tablespoons fresh white breadcrumbs**
**3 tablespoons grated Parmigiano Reggiano**
**2 tablespoons pine nuts, roughly chopped**
**1 tablespoon olive oil, plus extra for drizzling**
**sea salt and freshly ground black pepper**

**Serves 6**

Preheat the oven to 180°C/160°C fan/350°F/gas 4.

Cut the courgettes in half lengthways. Blanch them in a saucepan of simmering salted water for 3 minutes, then drain and refresh in a bowl of iced water until cool. Scoop out the middle from each courgette.

Mash the ricotta in a bowl and season with salt and pepper. Stir in the eggs, garlic, basil and lemon zest.

In a separate bowl, combine the breadcrumbs, Parmigiano Reggiano and pine nuts.

Brush the courgettes with the olive oil, season and place on a baking sheet. Divide the ricotta mixture between the courgettes, spooning it into the cavities, and top with the cheesy breadcrumbs. Drizzle each courgette half with a little more oil, then bake in the preheated oven for 25–30 minutes until golden and crunchy. Serve hot or warm.

*The northern Apennines in the province of Bologna are a patchwork of cultivated fields, shrubby habitats and woodland, where wild boar can be found.*

# BAKED BABY PEPPERS

## PEPPERONI AL FORNO

*So attractive, so incredibly tasty. Best enjoyed in the season of peppers during the summer.*

8 baby red peppers, cut in half lengthways, core and seeds removed
40 g/1½ oz. coarse fresh white breadcrumbs
2 tablespoons small capers, rinsed and chopped
2 garlic cloves, crushed
2 large handfuls of chopped fresh flat-leaf parsley
handful of chopped fresh mint
3 tablespoons freshly grated Pecorino
225 ml/scant 1 cup dry white wine
4 tablespoons olive oil
sea salt and freshly ground black pepper

**Serves 4**

Preheat the oven to 200°C/180°C fan/400°F/gas 6. Grease a shallow ovenproof dish or roasting tray.

Arrange the halved peppers in the prepared dish, skin-side down, in a single layer.

Sprinkle over the breadcrumbs, capers, garlic, parsley, mint, cheese and some salt and pepper. Spoon over the wine, then drizzle with the oil. Cover the dish or tray with foil and bake in the preheated oven for 30 minutes.

Remove the foil, return the dish to the oven and bake for a further 30 minutes, or until the peppers are charred. Leave to cool for 15 minutes before serving.

# BAKED ONIONS STUFFED WITH PROSCIUTTO

## CIPOLLE RIPIENI

*Delicious onions, filled with a breadcrumb stuffing that is flavoured with prosciutto and Grana Padano, and baked until sweet and tender. I like to serve them as an* antipasto.

**6–8 large white onions, peeled**
**2 tablespoons coarse fresh white breadcrumbs**
**1/2 tablespoon milk**
**150 g/5 1/2 oz. prosciutto, finely chopped**
**6 tablespoons grated Grana Padano**
**1 medium egg, beaten**
**15 g/1 tablespoon unsalted butter, cubed, plus extra to grease**
**sea salt and freshly ground black pepper**

**Serves 6–8**

Add the onions to a pan of boiling salted water and simmer for 15 minutes.

Meanwhile, moisten the breadcrumbs with the milk.

Preheat the oven to 180°C/160°C fan/350°F/gas 4.

Drain the onions, reserving the cooking liquid, then pat the onions dry with paper towels. Cut a thin slice from the top of each onion and scoop out the insides using a teaspoon, reserving half of the onion flesh that has been removed. Place the hollowed-out onion shells, upside down, on a board while you prepare the filling.

Finely chop the reserved onion flesh and place in a bowl. Squeeze the breadcrumbs to remove any excess moisture, then add to the bowl with the onion.

Add the prosciutto, Grana Padano and beaten egg, then season with salt and pepper and mix well. Spoon the stuffing into the onion shells.

Grease a baking dish with butter. Arrange the stuffed onions in the dish with the butter. Moisten the onions with about 50 ml/3 1/2 tablespoons of the reserved cooking liquid.

Bake in the preheated oven for 40 minutes, basting the onions regularly with juices from the pan. Serve hot.

## CARAMELIZED ONIONS

### FRIGGIONE

*Humble, delightful and full of rich history. It has been said that 'eating bread and onions means just getting by', but both peasant and aristocracy have loved them since the 14th century. I was first alerted to this dish by a student who I have known for two decades, Deborah Wong. Thank you.*

**1 kg/2¼ lb. white onions, thinly sliced**
**50 g/¼ cup golden/raw caster/ superfine sugar**
**60 ml/¼ cup olive oil**
**400 g/14 oz. can plum tomatoes**
**7 g/1½ teaspoons sea salt**
**honey, to sweeten (optional)**

**Serves 4–6**

Place the sliced onions in a large bowl. Pour in enough cold water to cover and stir in half the sugar. Leave to rest for 45 minutes. Drain and repeat with fresh water and the remaining sugar, then rest for a further 45 minutes.

Heat the olive oil in a large pan over a low heat. Add the drained onions and cook slowly, stirring from time to time, for 1 hour with the lid on so the onions release their sweetness.

Add the tomatoes and cook uncovered for a further 25 minutes to evaporate the liquid. Season with salt and pepper, and add a little honey if you want more sweetness.

Simmer for 1 hour, topping up the liquid if necessary.

Serve the onions warm with some good rustic bread or on crostini.

## FRITTATA WITH SPRING ONIONS

### FRITTATA DI CIPOLOTTO

*Including this recipe in this chapter generated something of a debate. 'Is it really interesting enough?' Providing all the ingredients used are in the peak of perfection, then the answer is yes, it is! The addition of balsamic vinegar to serve is a big surprise. I enjoyed this on a whirlwind trip to Osteria dell'Oroa in the university district of Bologna. The onion has always been the queen of a poor man's kitchen, but also a favourite of the wealthy – a real expression of Bologna.*

**2 tablespoons olive oil**
**6 spring onions/scallions, sliced on the diagonal into 1-cm/½-inch pieces**
**6 large/US extra-large eggs**
**sea salt and freshly ground black pepper**
**½ tablespoon balsamic vinegar, to finish**

**Serves 4–6**

Heat the olive oil in a large frying pan/skillet. Add the spring onions and cook over a medium heat for 5–7 minutes, or until the onion is softened and just golden.

Beat the eggs in a bowl and season with salt and pepper. Add the eggs to the pan and cook for 7–8 minutes on each side.

Slide the frittata onto a large plate and drizzle with balsamic vinegar just before serving.

**Note:** *I often cook this frittata just on one side, then transfer it to an oven preheated to 180°C/160°C fan/350°F/gas 4 for 6 minutes just to set the top.*

# AUBERGINE, TOMATO & PARMIGIANO REGGIANO BAKE

## MELANZANE ALLA PARMIGIANA

*There are many recipes for this classic dish, which is eaten and enjoyed all over Italy. This is a real family favourite that is so simple to make; I have taught this recipe to many people, including in Italy! Other recipes include mozzarella, but in this delicious variation from Modena, it is the egg that forms the binding.*

**4 aubergines/eggplant, cut into 5-mm/1/8-inch thick slices**
**1 kg/2 1/4 lb. plum tomatoes, roughly chopped**
**2 garlic cloves, crushed**
**6 tablespoons olive oil**
**2 tablespoons tomato purée/paste**
**100 g/1 cup grated Parmigiano Reggiano**
**20 g/3/4 oz. fresh basil leaves, torn**
**1 large/US extra-large egg, beaten**
**sea salt and freshly ground black pepper**

*20-cm/8-inch square ovenproof baking dish*

**Serves 6**

Preheat the oven to 200°/180°C fan/400°F/gas 6.

Set a colander over a plate and layer the aubergine slices in it, sprinkling a little salt between each layer. Set aside for 20 minutes, then rinse and drain. Pat dry with paper towels.

Meanwhile, in a shallow pan, mix together the tomatoes, garlic and 2 tablespoons of the olive oil. Cover and cook over a high heat for 5 minutes. Uncover and reduce the heat, then cook, stirring continuously, for 8 minutes. Pass the tomato mixture through a sieve/strainer and discard the seeds and skin. Stir in the tomato purée and adjust the seasoning to taste.

Lightly brush the aubergine slices with the remaining olive oil. Heat a griddle or frying pan/skillet over a high heat. Cook the aubergine slices, in batches if necessary, for 5–7 minutes until well browned. Remove from the pan and leave to drain on paper towels.

Lay a few of the aubergine slices in the bottom of the baking dish. Spoon over some of the tomato sauce, sprinkle with grated Parmiggiano Reggiano and scatter over a few basil leaves. Repeat with the remaining ingredients to build up more layers.

Pour the beaten egg over the top, sprinkle over a little more cheese and bake in the preheated oven for 30 minutes until the topping is golden.

# CAULIFLOWER, ARTICHOKES, LEEKS & BROCCOLI BRAISED IN BALSAMIC VINEGAR

## VERDURE STUFATE ALL'ACETO BALSAMICO

*This is my idea of food heaven with the vegetables all taking centre stage. This particular combination should be enjoyed in the artichoke season, whether it's March or September – the* secondo fiore *of the artichokes is well worth the wait. This recipe is a celebration of seasonal vegetables and the region's amazing balsamic vinegar.*

**1 small cauliflower, core removed**
**3 fresh bay leaves**
**4 small artichokes**
**juice of 1 lemon**
**2 tablespoons olive oil**
**120 g/4½ oz. pancetta, smoked or unsmoked, diced**
**2 leeks, cleaned and roughly chopped, white only**
**250 g/9 oz. broccoli (preferably purple sprouting), tough stems removed and roughly chopped**
**60 ml/¼ cup homemade broth (any type; see pages 40–41)**
**4 tablespoons extra virgin olive oil**
**2 tablespoons best-quality balsamic vinegar**
**handful of fresh flat-leaf parsley, roughly chopped**
**sea salt and freshly ground black pepper**

**Serves 4**

Parboil the cauliflower in a saucepan of boiling salted water for about 10 minutes. I like to add fresh bay leaves, ripped a little to release their flavour, to the water. Drain the cauliflower, separate into individual florets and set aside.

Peel the artichoke stems and remove the tough outer leaves. Trim the stems, cut the artichokes in half lengthways and remove the chokes with a teaspoon. Cut each half into 4 slices and immediately place in a bowl of water acidulated with lemon juice to prevent discolouration.

Heat the olive oil in a generously sized frying pan/skillet and gently fry the pancetta over a medium heat.

Meanwhile, drain the artichokes.

Increase the heat and add the cauliflower, artichokes, leeks and broccoli and sauté for 5 minutes. Pour in the broth, season well with salt and pepper and cook for 3–4 minutes or until the broth has been completely absorbed.

Drizzle with extra virgin olive oil and balsamic vinegar, then garnish with the chopped parsley. Serve either hot or warm.

**Note:** *The pancetta can easily be omitted to create a vegetarian version of this dish.*

# TWELFTH NIGHT STUFFED SAVOY CABBAGE

## VERZOLINI DELLA VIGILIA

*In Italy, the festive celebrations draw to a close with the Twelfth Night on January 5th. This dish of stuffed Savoy cabbage leaves is traditionally served after midnight as part of a celebration meal. Other regions celebrate with different foods, but in Emilia-Romagna, the humble cabbage is transformed into this simple yet effective vegetable dish.*

**2 slices of stale country style bread**
**125 ml/½ cup milk**
**1 large Savoy cabbage, leaves separated (you should get roughly 30 large leaves)**
**75 g/2½ oz. stale breadcrumbs**
**75 g/¾ cup grated Grana Padano**
**2 large/US extra-large eggs, beaten**
**50 g/3½ tablespoons unsalted butter**
**2 tablespoons olive oil**
**1 onion, finely chopped**
**2 tablespoons tomato purée/paste**
**1 litre/4 cups vegetable broth (see page 40)**
**fresh flat-leaf parsley, to garnish**
**sea salt and freshly ground black pepper**

**Serves 6–8**

Place the slices of bread in a bowl, cover with the milk and leave to soak for about 12 minutes.

Cook the cabbage leaves in a large saucepan of boiling salted water for 6–7 minutes, then drain. Choose 24 of the largest leaves and set aside. Finely shred the remaining leaves.

Squeeze the bread to remove any moisture and place in a bowl with the shredded cabbage, breadcrumbs, grated cheese, eggs and some salt and pepper. Mix until all the ingredients are well combined.

Place a dollop of the stuffing mixture in the centre of one of the large cabbage leaves, then fold up like an envelope to enclose the stuffing. Use a cocktail stick to secure the parcel if needed. Repeat with the rest of the cabbage leaves and remaining stuffing.

To make the sauce, melt the butter in a saucepan, add the oil, then add the onion and gently fry for 6 minutes until softened and golden. Stir the tomato purée into the broth and then pour the broth into the pan. Season with salt and pepper and mix well.

Place the stuffed cabbage leaves in a shallow casserole dish/Dutch oven with a lid in a single layer (use two dishes if needed) and pour over the sauce. Cook gently on the hob over a low heat for 20 minutes with the lid on. Garnish with chopped parsley immediately before serving.

**Note:** *The stuffed cabbage parcels can be made ahead of time and refrigerated until needed. Having them prepared and ready to cook can be a real help during the festive period, which can be cooking chaos.*

# PAN-FRIED COURGETTES

## ZUCCHINI TRIFOLATI

*On my visit to Bologna, the vegetables in the Mercato delle Erbe were in full stride. What I really appreciated was all the different varieties of courgettes/zucchini on offer. I always recommend young courgettes as the best for cooking using this method. Larger courgettes are better filled and baked.* Trifolati *is a method of slicing and cooking in olive oil with garlic and parsley. Other ingredients may be added at the cook's discretion.*

**2 tablespoons olive oil, for cooking**
**350 g/12 oz. young courgettes/ zucchini, washed and cut into 2.5-cm/1-inch rounds**
**3 garlic cloves, thinly sliced**
**200 g/8 oz. ripe cherry tomatoes, cut in half horizontally**
**handful of fresh parsley leaves**
**handful of fresh basil leaves**
**1 tablespoon best-quality extra virgin olive oil, preferably fresh and fruity, for drizzling**
**sea salt and freshly ground black pepper**

**Serves 4–6**

Heat the olive oil in a frying pan/skillet over a medium heat. Add the courgettes and garlic and stir well, then season with salt and pepper.

When the courgettes begin to brown, add the tomatoes, stir well and cook for about 7–9 minutes until the courgettes are lightly golden.

Scatter over the parsley and basil, then drizzle with the extra virgin olive oil to finish just before serving.

*The Church of Saint Apollinaris, with its distinctive clock tower, sits in the fortified village of Castello di Serravalle.*

CHAPTER SIX

# DESSERTS
## Dolci

*Levizzano Rangone Castle sits in the hills of the Lambrusco Grasparossa in Modena, surrounded by vineyards that produce the region's famous Lambrusco wine.*

# A SWEET TOOTH

I HAVE TO ADMIT that the Italians have a very sweet tooth. It's been a national characteristic ever since the Venetians began to deal in sugar (as well as spices, chocolate and coffee) around the beginning of the twelfth century. Italian cooks very quickly learned how to refine sugar and use this 'white gold'. They became proficient in inventing and producing sweetmeats of all kinds. For centuries, the Italians were known across Europe for their expertise in desserts, pastries and sweets/candies; a rich household in nineteenth-century England might have employed a French chef, but they would have insisted on an Italian confectioner.

Even today, the Italians love their daily consumption of sweet things, ranging from sweet breads, cakes, tarts, pastries and biscuits/cookies, to creamy puddings, ice creams, sorbets and candies. There are *pasticcerie* (cake shops) in every town and village. Little sweet treats are enjoyed with a morning cup of coffee (some might even be eaten for breakfast), as well as lunch or in the middle of the afternoon. No right-minded Italian visiting friends or family would set off without a few (preferably home-made) biscuits – such as my *amaretti* (see page 171) – as a gift. You could not have an Italian wedding, christening, confirmation, birthday or saint's day without celebratory cakes and biscuits in abundance.

During Carnevale (or carnival, which comes from the Latin for 'farewell to meat'), revelers feast on the foods that are to be avoided during Lent. *Carnevale* lasts two weeks, but the final few days are the most important: the days from *giovedi Grasso* (Fat Thursday) until *martedi Grasso* (Fat Tuesday) allow for a lot of over-indulgence.... *Bombolini*, doughnuts filled with custard, are very popular at carnival time, but slightly tricky to eat. I offer something a little bit different here: a fried ricotta puff (see page 179), which is the perfect nibble when you are in the middle of carnival with your mask on, rushing to the next delight. Likewise, *sfrappole* (or *frappe*, see page 187) are classic carnival fare, probably best known in Emilia-Romagna: they are deep-fried thin ribbons of sweet pastry, dusted with icing sugar.

Pasta dough is sometimes used in sweet things. The dough can be made with powdered sugar and grated orange zest, then cut into tagliatelle and deep-fried. There is also something called a *torta di tagliatelle*, which comes from Ferrara: it has a base of shortcrust pastry, a filling of macarons and ground almonds and a topping of fresh egg pasta ribbons, usually the thinner *tagliolini* rather than *tagliatelle*. It is then baked like a tart. What I have given you here, though, is *ravioli dolci* (see page 179): sweet pasta parcels enclosing a generous amount of fruit spread, which are shaped into half moons and baked. These sweet ravioli are associated with March 19th, the feast day of St. Joseph and Father's Day in Italy. Also made with a sweet dough is the local speciality *pinza Bolognese*, which is filled with mostarda Bolognese, a sweet thick spread made from quince.

I have included a recipe for *pasta frolla* (shortcrust pasty), which can be used to make many delicious things. A typical dessert of Bologna is the *torta di riso* (see page 184), a rice cake that is traditionally prepared during the *Festa degli Addobbi* (Festival of Decorations). Originating in the fifteenth century, this festival occurs every 10 years when precious church possessions are paraded through the streets and houses are decorated with flags and ribbons. The *torta di riso* is integral to these celebrations. I have added another dimension to it by encasing it in shortcrust pastry.

Cakes, either to accompany coffee and tea or served for dessert, are important in Emilia-Romagna. *Panspeziale* (literally 'special bread') is indeed special, not least because of its interesting history. It was first made by apothecaries who used *spezie* (spices) in medications. The *Certosini* (Carthusian monks) then took over the baking, hence the alternative name, *certosino*. Dense with candied fruit and nuts, this cake is a favourite at Christmas (see page 168). As is *ciambella Romagnola* (see page 172), a breakfast cake coated with pearl sugar, which is perfect dipped into your morning coffee. The chocolate cake most famous here is *panpepato*, a dense, dark, spiced fruit and nut cake, served at Christmas in Ferrara. Mine is a little lighter (see page 187).

I haven't given you any custard-type desserts here, as I have done so elsewhere, but there are two which deserve mention as they are very popular in Emilia-Romagna: *zuppa inglese* and *zabaione*. The first is an Italian version of British trifle, while the second is the

Italian concoction of egg yolks, sugar and Marsala. *Zabaione* is common all over Italy, but in Bologna it is raised to new heights, baked into cakes and sweet breads, used in or on ice creams, spooned into coffee, and offered instead of cream with fruit as a dessert. The only custard I have allowed myself here is the one that forms the basis of my vanilla ice cream (see page 188). There are many *gelaterie* (ice-cream shops) throughout Emilia-Romagna. The region has openly declared its passion for home-made ice creams through a museum dedicated to gelato and by opening a university to train ice-cream makers. The Carpigiani Gelato University opened in 2003, in Bologna, and sends its graduates to professional kitchens throughout the world.

Finally, we come to the region's liqueurs. The best known is *nocino* from Modena, made from unripe green walnuts; traditionally associated with the Festa di San Giovanni (St. John the Baptist) on June 24th. Others are made from hazelnuts, sloes and even dandelions. Here I give a recipe for a liqueur made from lemon verbena (see page 176). The plant comes from South America, but grows well in colder climes if protected from winter frosts. Lemon verbena is usually steeped in hot water to make a tea, but also makes an interesting liqueur.

# CHRISTMAS CAKE FROM BOLOGNA

## CERTOSINO DI BOLOGNA (O PANSPEZIALE)

Panspeziale *is the cake made in Bologna at Christmas time, and very 'special' it is too. The recipe was created by the monks of Certosa, who made it for the Cardinal Lambertini. Like other classic Christmas cakes, it should be made about a month in advance of the festive season to truly develop all of the flavours.*

**250 g/1¼ cups raisins**
**3 tablespoons Marsala**
**5 tablespoons fragrant honey**
**225 g/1 cup caster/superfine sugar**
**85 g/⅓ cup/¾ stick unsalted butter**
**1 tablespoon fennel seeds or aniseeds**
**1 tablespoon ground cinnamon**
**115 g/4 oz. dark/bittersweet chocolate with 50% cocoa solids, coarsely chopped**
**6 eating apples, peeled, cored and grated**
**115 g/4 oz. candied orange peel, chopped**
**225 g/1⅔ cups blanched almonds, coarsely chopped**
**115 g/¾ cup pine nuts**
**500 g/3¾ cups plain/all-purpose flour or Italian 00 flour**
**½ teaspoon baking powder**

TO FINISH

**3 tablespoons apricot jam/preserve, warmed**
**selection of crystallized/candied fruit, such as oranges, lemons, apricots and cherries**
**50 g/½ cup whole blanched toasted almonds**

*23-cm/9-inch round, loose-bottomed, deep cake pan*

**Serves 12–16**

Soak the raisins in the Marsala for at least 30 minutes, preferably overnight.

Preheat the oven to 180°C/160°C fan/350°F/gas 4. Grease the cake pan and line the base and sides with parchment paper.

Heat the honey, sugar, butter and 2 tablespoons water together in a saucepan until the sugar dissolves.

Crush the fennel seeds or aniseeds and add to the pan along with the cinnamon. Pour the mixture into a large mixing bowl.

Add the Marsala-soaked raisins, chocolate, apples, orange peel, almonds, pine nuts, flour and baking powder to the bowl and mix well together.

Scrape the mixture into the prepared cake pan and bake for about 1¼ hours, or until a skewer inserted in the centre comes out clean. Leave to cool in the pan for 15 minutes before turning out on to a wire rack and leaving to cool completely.

Tightly wrap the cake in parchment paper and then foil and store for a month before decorating the cake.

To decorate, brush the top of the cake with two-thirds of the apricot jam, then stud the surface with the crystallized fruit and almonds in whatever pattern you prefer. Finally, brush the top of the cake, including the fruit and almonds, with the remaining jam.

# ORANGE, GRAPEFRUIT & TANGERINE AMARETTI

## AMARETTI ALL'ARANCIA, POMPELMO E MANDARINO

*Over the years, I've written so very many recipes for amaretti, each one slightly different to suit a certain time of year or occasion. This is my autumn/fall amaretti, so light and refreshing, perfect with an espresso. I enjoyed this version while on a business trip to Bologna – the recipe was willingly given to me, scribbled on a napkin.*

**2 large/US extra-large egg whites**
**200 g/1 cup golden/raw caster/superfine sugar**
**250 g/2½ cups ground almonds (freshly ground if possible)**
**½ teaspoon baking powder**
**1 tablespoon orange juice**
**zest of 1 unwaxed orange**
**zest of 1 unwaxed grapefruit**
**zest of 1 unwaxed tangerine**
**½ teaspoon vanilla extract**
**½ teaspoon sea salt flakes, crumbled**
**25 g/1 oz. white unpeeled almonds**

TO FINISH
**2 tablespoons caster/superfine sugar**
**2 tablespoons icing/confectioners' sugar**

**Makes 25**

Preheat the oven to 170°C/150°C fan/325°F/gas 3. Line two baking sheets with parchment paper.

In a grease-free bowl, whisk the egg whites until firm peaks form. Add all the remaining ingredients (except the sugars and almonds to finish) and mix well. The dough should feel damp.

Shape small amounts of the dough into chestnut-size balls. Roll each ball, first in the caster sugar and then the icing sugar.

Press a whole almond into the top of each ball to flatten it slightly and create cracks on the surface.

Place the amaretti on the lined baking sheets and bake in the preheated oven for 14 minutes until golden brown.

Leave to cool on a wire rack, then dust with a little more icing sugar to finish.

# ITALIAN BREAKFAST CAKE

## CIAMBELLA ROMAGNOLA

*A classic, simple sponge cake with a refreshing lemony taste is baked in a ring-shaped cake pan and decorated with pearl sugar, which gives a contrasting crunchy texture. Due to its characteristic shape, it is also known as a Bolognese Ring.*

**2 tablespoons pearl sugar**
**butter or baking spray, for greasing**
**150 g/2/3 cup/1 1/4 sticks unsalted butter**
**250 g/2 cups Italian 00 flour**
**1 1/2 teaspoons baking powder**
**pinch of sea salt**
**zest of 2 unwaxed lemons**
**125 g/scant 2/3 cup golden/raw caster/superfine sugar**
**4 large/US extra-large eggs, separated**
**125 ml/1/2 cup whole/full-fat milk**
**2 teaspoons vanilla extract**

TO SERVE
**crème fraîche or whipped cream**
**selection of summer berries**

*25-cm/10-inch bundt/tube cake pan*

**Serves 10–12**

Spray the bundt cake pan with baking spray or use a brush to grease the pan. Sprinkle half the pearl sugar over the bottom of the pan.

Preheat the oven to 180°C/160°C fan/350°F/gas 4.

Melt the butter and set aside until needed.

In a bowl, whisk together the flour, baking powder, salt and lemon zest and set aside.

In a separate bowl, whisk the egg whites until soft peaks form.

In another separate bowl, add the sugar and beat in the egg yolks one at a time. Gradually fold in the flour mixture, bit by bit, then add the melted butter and stir to combine. Add the milk and vanilla extract, then mix well.

Finally, add the egg whites, one-third at a time, mixing lightly between each addition.

Pour the cake batter into the prepared mould or pan, then level and smooth the surface. Sprinkle the remaining pearl sugar on the surface.

Bake in the preheated oven for 40–45 minutes until a skewer or toothpick inserted into centre of the cake comes out clean.

Leave to cool in the tin for 10 minutes before turning out onto a wire rack to cool completely. Serve slices with a spoonful of crème fraîche or whipped cream and a handful of summer berries.

# PEACH & STRAWBERRY TART

## CROSTATA CON PESCHE E FRAGOLE

*While I was testing recipes for this book, the peach season was in full stride. This tart is a beautiful combination of textures, flavours and colours. I heartily recommend.*

**4 ripe peaches, stoned/pitted and sliced**
**300 g/10½ oz. firm strawberries, hulled and halved**
**2 tablespoons apricot jam / preserve**

PASTRY (*PASTA FROLLA*)
**250 g/2 cups Italian 00 flour or white spelt flour, plus extra for dusting**
**75 g/¾ cup icing/confectioners' sugar, plus extra for dusting**
**125 g/½ cup plus 1 tablespoon chilled unsalted butter**
**1 large/US extra-large egg**
**pinch of salt**
**few drops of vanilla extract**
**grated zest of unwaxed 1 lemon**

*23-cm/9-inch springform cake pan*

**Serves 6–8**

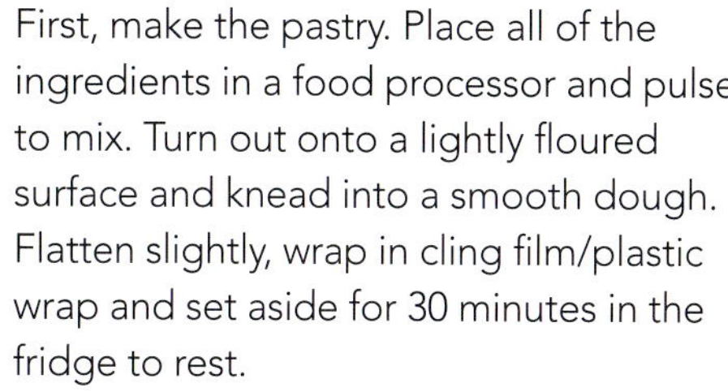

First, make the pastry. Place all of the ingredients in a food processor and pulse to mix. Turn out onto a lightly floured surface and knead into a smooth dough. Flatten slightly, wrap in cling film/plastic wrap and set aside for 30 minutes in the fridge to rest.

Preheat the oven to 180°C/160°C fan/350°F/gas 4. Grease and flour the springform cake pan.

Combine the peaches and strawberries in a bowl and set aside.

Roll the pastry dough into a 30-cm/12-inch circle. Make sure the outer edge of the circle is neat.

Use the pastry to line the prepared cake pan, making sure that the pastry is snug to the edge, but without stretching it too much as the pastry will shrink back during cooking. Allow the excess pastry to overhang the sides of the pan.

Add the fruit to the pastry case, then fold the overhanging pastry down over the fruit to form an even border – but the fruit should still be visible in the centre. Bake in the preheated oven for 35–40 minutes until golden and crisp. Leave to cool completely on a wire rack.

Heat the apricot jam in a saucepan, then brush over the fruit filling to glaze. Dust with icing sugar if desired to finish.

# LEMON VERBENA LIQUEUR

## LIQUORE DI CEDRINA

*I grow lemon verbena in my garden, which I use to make this liqueur – a natural digestif and a favourite throughout the Emilia-Romagna region. It has a zingy flavour, but is quite potent, so do drink responsibly.*

**10 large sprigs of lemon verbena (freshly picked if possible)**
**700 g/3½ cups golden/raw caster/superfine sugar**
**zest of 3 unwaxed lemons**
**1 litre/4 cups vodka**
**650 ml/2⅔ cups distilled water**

*2-litre/quart glass jar with a tight-fitting lid*
*glass bottles with a swing-top seal or screw cap lid*

**Makes 1.5 litres/ 50 fl oz./1.5 quarts**

Remove any woody stems from the lemon verbena sprigs, then place them in the large glass jar along with the sugar and lemon zest. Pour in the vodka and water, making sure the lemon verbena sprigs are submerged. Tightly seal the jar, then set aside in a cool, dark place for 2 weeks.

After the liqueur has been left to infuse for 2 weeks, shake the jar to agitate all the ingredients. Strain the leaves, zest and any sediment from the liqueur by passing it through a muslin cloth or fine-mesh strainer. Discard the contents of the cloth or strainer.

Using a funnel, divide the liqueur between airtight glass bottles with a good seal (add a fresh sprig of lemon verbena if liked). Close the bottles, then set aside in a cool, dark place for 2 months. After 2 months, the flavours of the liqueur will have mellowed.

*Ricotta is used in both sweet and savoury dishes across Italy with great affection. Made from the whey of Parmesan cheese, here ricotta is made into something rather glamorous,* Bomboloni.

## CHOCOLATE & ORANGE RICOTTA PUFFS

### BOMBOLONI

**500 g/1 lb. 2 oz. firm, fresh ricotta**
**55 g/¼ cup caster/superfine sugar**
**3 large/US extra-large eggs**
**2 tablespoons orange liqueur**
**2 teaspoons finely grated orange zest**
**95 g/3 oz. dark/bittersweet chocolate chips**
**150 g/generous 1 cup plain/all-purpose flour**
**2 teaspoons baking powder**
**vegetable oil, for deep-frying**
**icing/confectioners' sugar, for dusting**

**Makes about 35**

Whisk together the ricotta, caster sugar, eggs, orange liqueur and orange zest in a large bowl until well combined. Stir in the chocolate chips. Sift in the flour and baking powder, then lightly fold until just combined. Chill the mixture in the fridge for 30 minutes.

Heat the oil in a large heavy-based saucepan over a high heat.

Working in batches to avoid overcrowding the pan, carefully drop tablespoons of the mixture into the hot oil and deep fry until golden and puffed. Remove the cooked puffs with a slotted spoon and drain on paper towels. Dust with sifted icing sugar to finish.

## SWEET RAVIOLI FILLED WITH FRUIT PURÉE

### RAVIOLI DOLCI

*These fruit-filled ravioli are a classic for Carnevale in Italy. The traditional version is often filled with a sweet ricotta, but the filling can really be altered and amended to your particular tastes.*

DOUGH

**360 g/2¾ cups Italian 00 flour**
**½ teaspoon sea salt**
**30 g/2 tablespoons caster/superfine sugar**
**½ teaspoon dried yeast**
**45 g/3 tablespoons unsalted butter, melted**
**220 ml/scant 1 cup whole/full-fat milk**
**115 ml/scant ½ cup body temperature water**
**30 g/2 tablespoons polenta**

FILLING

**120 g/4½ oz. fruit purée (I like apricot or quince)**
**icing/confectioners' sugar, for dusting**

**Makes 20–24**

In a large bowl, add the flour, salt, sugar and yeast and mix well. Make a well in the flour and add the melted butter, milk and enough water to create a damp dough. The dough should be neither wet nor dry, just damp, so adjust the amount of flour and water as needed, depending on the flour type and time of year. Wrap the dough in cling film/plastic wrap and leave to rest in the fridge for 30 minutes.

Preheat the oven to 200°C/ 180°C fan/400°F/gas 6.

Sprinkle the polenta over two large baking sheets. Roll out the dough into two large rectangles, 3 mm/⅛ inch thick. Using an 8 cm/3-inch round cutter, punch out lots of discs from the dough.

Using a teaspoon, put a small mound of fruit purée on one half of each disc. Fold in half over the filling to make a half-moon shape. Press to seal.

Bake the ravioli in the oven for 15 minutes until golden. Dust with sifted icing sugar to finish.

# BLUEBERRY & LEMON CAKE

## TORTA DI MIRTILLI E LIMONE

*The perfect cake during summer when blueberries are at their peak. At other times of the year, feel free to use the cake recipe as a base and add in other seasonal fruit, such as raspberries, gooseberries, blackberries and figs.*

**175 g/3/4 cup/1 1/2 sticks unsalted butter, plus extra for greasing**
**175 g/scant 1 cup golden/raw caster/superfine sugar**
**3 large/US extra-large eggs**
**2 teaspoons vanilla bean paste**
**zest of 2 unwaxed lemons (use the juice for the syrup, see below)**
**200 g/1 1/2 cups Italian 00 flour**
**1/2 teaspoon salt**
**1 1/2 teaspoons baking powder**
**200 g/7 oz. blueberries (or other fruits in season)**

SYRUP
**juice of 2 lemons**
**2 tablespoons golden/raw caster/superfine sugar**

*20-cm/8-inch round, loose-bottomed cake pan*

**Serves 8–10**

Preheat the oven to 180°C/160°C fan/350°F/gas 4. Grease the cake pan and line the base and sides with parchment paper.

Using an electric stand mixer or handheld mixer, cream the butter and sugar together really well until light, fluffy and pale yellow. This is the most important stage and its vital you take your time with it.

Add the eggs, one at a time, beating well between each addition. Stir in the vanilla paste and lemon zest, then lightly fold in the flour, salt and baking powder just until there are no visible pockets of dry flour. Scrape the cake mixture into the prepared cake pan.

Scatter the blueberries evenly over the top of the cake and bake in the preheated oven for 35 minutes until golden and well risen. Leave to cool in the pan on a wire rack.

While the cake is baking, make the syrup. Warm the lemon juice and sugar in a small saucepan until all the sugar has dissolved, then simmer for 2–3 minutes.

Spoon the syrup over the cooled cake and allow it to soak in, then remove from the pan before slicing and serving.

# RICE PUDDING TARTS

## TORTINI DI RISO BOLOGNESE

*I had the idea to adapt the basic recipe for Bologna's* torta di riso *by baking the cake mixture inside tart cases made from* pasta frolla, *which worked incredibly well.*

**1 quantity Pastry (*Pasta Frolla*; see page 175), wrapped in cling film/plastic wrap and rested for 30 minutes in the fridge**
**120 g/⅔ cup arborio rice**
**900 ml/3¾ cups whole/full-fat milk**
**100 g/½ cup golden/raw caster/superfine sugar**
**2 large/US extra-large eggs**
**zest of 1 unwaxed lemon**
**2 teaspoons vanilla extract**
**60 ml/¼ cup double/heavy cream**
**60 g/½ cup chopped toasted almonds**
**2 teaspoons brandy or Marsala**
**handful of flaked almonds**
**icing/confectioners' sugar, for dusting**

*12-hole muffin pan*

**Serves 8**

Put the rice and milk in a saucepan and cook over a low heat for 15–18 minutes or until the rice has softened. Transfer to a bowl and leave to cool.

Preheat the oven to 180°C/160°C fan/350°F/gas 4. Grease eight of the holes of the muffin pan with butter.

Add the sugar, eggs, cream, almonds, brandy or Marsala, lemon zest and vanilla extract to the rice mixture, then stir to mix well.

Roll out the chilled pastry dough to 5-mm/¼-inch thick. Using a round cutter slightly larger than the holes of the muffin pan, press out 8 discs from the pastry. Press the pastry discs into wthe greased holes of the muffin pan.

Fill the pastry cases with the cold rice pudding and then scatter a few flaked almonds over the top of each tart.

Bake the tarts for 25 minutes until crisp and golden. Remove the tarts from the muffin pan, leave to cool, then dust with icing sugar.

*Bologna's iconic two towers, Asinelli and Garisenda, stand tall over the historic city.*

# CHOCOLATE CAKE

## TORTA DI CIOCCOLATO

*Over the years, I have written nearly 50 recipes for chocolate cake in the pursuit of the perfect balance of flavours. Made with brandy-soaked raisins, this is a dream of a chocolate cake.*

**100 g/½ cup/1 stick unsalted butter**
**175 g/scant 1 cup caster/superfine sugar**
**3 large/US extra-large eggs, separated**
**2 tablespoons milk**
**200 g/1½ cups Italian 00 flour**
**2 teaspoons baking powder**
**50 g/½ cup unsweetened cocoa powder**
**30 g/¼ cup raisins, soaked in 2 tablespoons brandy**
**icing/confectioners' sugar, for dusting (optional)**

*20-cm/8-inch round cake pan*

**Serves 6–8**

Preheat the oven to 160°C/140°C fan/325°F/gas 3. Grease the cake pan and line the base and sides with parchment paper.

In an electric stand mixer, cream the butter and sugar until pale and fluffy. Add the egg yolks and milk and mix until well combined. In a separate bowl, whisk the egg whites until firm peaks form.

Add the flour, baking powder, cocoa powder and brandy-soaked raisins to the butter and sugar mixture and mix well with a metal spoon. Next, carefully add the egg whites and lightly fold into the mixture.

Scrape the cake mixture into the cake pan and bake for 35 minutes until well risen and a wooden toothpick inserted into the centre comes out clean. Dust the cake with icing sugar, if preferred, before slicing and serving.

# DEEP-FRIED PASTRY STRIPS

## SFRAPPOLE

*During Carnevale, when everyone dresses up in costume and wears a mask for the festival, this is a typical Bolognese dessert. Each family will add their own unique twist to the recipe to make it special to them, such as a change in shape or size or adding a different liqueur.*

**400 g/3 cups Italian 00 flour**
**3 egg yolks**
**50 g/3½ tablespoons unsalted butter**
**100 g/½ cup caster/superfine sugar**
**zest of 1 unwaxed lemon**
**15 ml/1 tablespoon brandy or aniseed-flavoured liqueur**
**pinch of salt**
**½ teaspoon baking power**
**icing/confectioners' sugar, for dusting**
**2 litres/8 cups oil, for deep-frying (I prefer groundnut oil)**

*fluted pastry cutter*

**Serves 6**

Combine all the ingredients in a large mixing bowl and knead together into a dough. You can soften the dough with a little milk, if needed. Leave to rest in the fridge for 1 hour.

On a lightly floured surface, roll out the dough as thin as possible, about 3 mm/⅛ inch thick. Using a sharp knife or fluted pastry cutter, cut the dough into strips, three fingers width wide, and as long as your pan will allow.

Heat the oil in a large, deep frying pan/skillet. Working in batches to avoid overcrowding the pan, fry the pastry strips until golden brown, roughly 90 seconds on each side. Drain on paper towels to absorb any excess oil, then dust with icing sugar. Enjoy while still warm.

# VANILLA ICE CREAM

## GELATO ALLA VANIGLIA

*When it comes to ice cream, vanilla is the purest flavour. This recipe is dedicated to mummy, the best gelato maker ever.*

**570 ml/2½ cups whole/full-fat milk**
**1 vanilla pod/bean, split lengthways**
**4 large/US extra-large egg yolks**
**200 g/1 cup golden/raw caster/superfine sugar**
**1 teaspoon vanilla extract**

*ice-cream machine (optional)*

**Serves 6**

Place 60 ml/¼ cup of the milk in a saucepan and scrape in the vanilla seeds. Place over a high heat to scald the milk.

Beat the egg yolks and sugar together in the top of a bain-marie or double boiler.

Scald the remaining milk in a separate pan and slowly mix into the egg mixture, stirring, to a thick custard consistency that coats the back of a spoon. Add the vanilla-infused milk.

Remove the bain-marie or double boiler from the heat and leave the mixture to cool, then chill in the fridge.

Stir the vanilla extract into the ice-cream, then freeze in an ice-cream machine or a freezer-safe container in the freezer, stirring every hour to break up any ice crystals and ensure the ice cream remains smooth.

# STRAWBERRY SORBET

## SORBETTO ALLA FRAGOLA

*This recipe was enjoyed in a local neighbourhood trattoria and had been missing from my repertoire. Enjoy in the height of strawberry season.*

**800 g/1¾ lb. ripe strawberries (preferably in season)**
**40 g/¼ cup golden/raw caster/superfine sugar**
**15 ml/1 tablespoon sweet dessert wine**
**juice of 1 lemon**
**1 large/US extra-large egg white**

*ice-cream machine (optional)*

**Serves 6**

Wash the strawberries and cut them into quarters. Put the strawberries, sugar, wine and lemon juice in a saucepan with 30 ml/2 tablespoons water, then bring to the boil to dissolve the sugar.

Transfer the strawberry mixture to a food processor and pulse until smooth. Leave to cool.

In a grease-free bowl, whisk the egg whites to form soft peaks, then fold into the cool strawberry purée.

Freeze in an ice-cream machine or a freezer-safe container in the freezer, stirring every hour to break up any ice crystals and ensure the sorbet remains smooth.

# INDEX

# PICTURE CREDITS

**9 above and below** awesome artt/Adobe Stock; **11** smash338/Adobe Stock; **12–13** Freesurf/Adobe Stock; **15 above left** dudlajzov/Adobe Stock; **15 above right** FV Photography/Adobe Stock; **15 below left** Luigi Bertello Photo - stock.adobe.com; **15 below centre** francescodemarco/Adobe Stock; **15 below right** Marina; **27** hungry_herbivore/Adobe Stock; **35** smash338/Adobe Stock; **36–37** dudlajzov/Adobe Stock; **39 above left** Luca Lorenzelli/Adobe Stock; **39 above centre** saragone/Adobe Stock; **39 above right** Vivida Photo PC/Adobe Stock; **39 below left** carinthian/Adobe Stock; **39 below right** Caterina Trimarchi/Adobe Stock; **46** petejeff/Adobe Stock; **50** SeanPavonePhoto/Adobe Stock; **67** smash338/Adobe Stock; **68–69** dudlajzov/Adobe Stock; **71 above right** Ekaterina Belova/Adobe Stock; **71 centre left** maurosessanta/Adobe Stock; **71 centre right** boryanam/Adobe Stock; **71 below left** effebi77/Adobe Stock; **77** Luca Lorenzilli/Adobe Stock; **105** frizio - stock.adobe.com; **107** smash338/Adobe Stock; **108–109** wjarek/Adobe Stock; **111 above left** Massimo Pizzotti/Adobe Stock; **111 above right** claudiozacc/Adobe Stock; **111 centre left** Fotokon - stock.adobe.com; **111 centre right** francescodemarco/Adobe Stock; **111 below left** Andrea Izzotti/Adobe Stock; **117** Salvatore Leanza/Adobe Stock; **118** ginettigino/Adobe Stock; **125** Renáta Sedmáková/Adobe Stock; **137** Vivida Photo PC/Adobe Stock; **139** smash338/Adobe Stock; **140–141** Aquarius/Adobe Stock; **143 above left** Paolo Gualdi/Adobe Stock; **143 above right** Giulio/Adobe Stock; **143 centre left** Fotokon - stock.adobe.com; **143 centre right** marcodeepsub/Adobe Stock; **143 below right** Giulio/Adobe Stock; **144** GiorgioMorara/Adobe Stock; **160** oltrelautostrada/Adobe Stock; **163** smash338/Adobe Stock; **164–165** stefanotermanini/Adobe Stock; **167 above left** frizio - stock.adobe.com; **167 above right** New Africa; **167 centre right** francescodemarco/Adobe Stock; **167 below left** Tomasz/Adobe Stock; **184** ronnybas/Adobe Stock

# ACKNOWLEDGEMENTS


Matteo Mansi, my dear friend, I'm so glad that we met, and your constant support means so much.

Julia Charles, for her sense of fun, humour and determination to produce beautiful books. Just joyful to work with.

Toni Kay, so gentle, kind, very diligent and with a wonderful knowledge of how to approach each subject with such love and understanding.

My dearest Abi Waters, for just simply everything. Her gentle, strong, kind ways are legendary and her attention to detail is absolutely, without question, vital. True happiness.

Food stylist, Kathy Kordalis – thank you for agreeing to do this project. Without your talent this book would not look as good as it does. And a huge thank you to your assistants on the shoot, Thanee Pass and Grace Jenkins.

Rita Platts – we were all very happy to be together on the photoshoot, working in your home. I noticed Rita's light tough and her understanding for each shot that developed over the course of the shoot to create this wonderful book.

Susan Fleming – our fifteenth project together! I cannot imagine this book without you. I just love our chats – they go off piste so frequently, but we get back on track eventually and create something truly special.

Lisa Pendreigh – for your expert eye and exceptional attention to detail.

Leslie Harrington – for overseeing the design. And Yvonne Doolan, unflappable Jack Duce and all at RPS for pulling this beautiful book together.

Of all the books I've ever written (of which there are many), this subject has been so tantalizing. I find life very dull when I'm not learning, so to say that I have learnt a lot is an understatement. I had to be very selective when choosing the recipes for this book as the food from the region is vast and far too much for just one book, but I have included the recipes that I found the most useful and delicious. I so hope you enjoy xxx